# Soaps and Suspects

# Soaps and Suspects

© Tandem Verlag GmbH, Birkenstraße 10, D-14469 Potsdam

Autorin: Uta Hasekamp
Muttersprachliches Korrektorat:
Context Gesellschaft für Sprachen- und Mediendienste mbH
Satz: Noch & Noch
Covergestaltung: Marlies Müller
Coverfoto: Shutterstock

Gesamtherstellung: Tandem Verlag GmbH
Alle Rechte vorbehalten
Wiedergabe – auch auszugsweise –
nur mit ausdrücklicher Genehmigung
durch den Verlag

ISBN 978-3-8427-0643-9

www.tandem-verlag.de

# Chapter 1

"It is a truth universally acknowledged[1] that a film production company in want of a location cannot do better than cast its eyes to St Stephen," read the first sentence of the article in St Stephen's local paper, the *East Yorkshire News*. "Filming of Balmaha Entertainment's TV-adaptation of Jane Austen's *Pride and Prejudice*[2] is to begin next week. The result, however, will not be yet another period film[3], but a sparky[4] contemporary take[5] on Britain's best-loved novel …"

Emilia Ramsay put down her coffee cup and picked up the newspaper to have a closer look. The article went on to list the locations that had been chosen, among them "the beautiful medieval church of St Stephen, and, in the historic centre of the town with the same name, a reputable art gallery specialising in 18th and 19th century English art. This gallery, in the new TV series *The Lives and Loves of the Bennet Sisters*, is owned by modern heroine[6] Elizabeth Bennet (played by delectable[7] soap opera star Nora Palliser) – and will be the very place where she encounters tall, dark and handsome Mr Darcy, impersonated by BAFTA[8] award-winner Ivor Byrnes."

Emilia sighed. In real life, the art gallery mentioned was owned by her partner Robert Rutherford and his ex-wife Stella Lloyd. Robert had been reluctant to make Lloyd Rutherford Fine Arts available to the film production company – but as Stella had, correctly, pointed out, there really was no alternative if they wanted to pay for the new security system the insurance company was insisting on. Stella had overseen the preproduction[9] stage at the gallery and had intended to be present during the filming, but just three days ago her mother had suffered a stroke[10] and she had had to travel to Devon.

Knowing that Robert was already dying a thousand deaths fearing for his precious pictures and would not be very well suited for the task, Emilia had volunteered to take over. With the help of her assistant Fiona Frommer her own business, the detective agency R&R Investigations (of which Robert was a partner), would be able to fend[11] for itself for a while. Besides, she could always take some work along and watching the filming

---

1 acknowledged: anerkannt  2 *Pride and Prejudice:* Roman (1813) von Jane Austen, dt. *Stolz und Vorurteil*
3 period film: Kostümfilm  4 sparky: frech und intelligent  5 contemporary take: moderne Interpretation
6 heroine: Heldin  7 delectable: (hier) reizvoll und sexy  8 BAFTA: British Academy of Film and Television Arts
9 preproduction: vor den Dreharbeiten  10 stroke: Schlaganfall  11 to fend for oneself: alleine zurechtkommen

was bound to be interesting. She only hoped that there would not be too much public interest after the newspaper article, passers-by[12] wanting to get a glimpse of Nora Palliser and Ivor Byrnes! But word would get out anyway …

The real-life vicar of the "beautiful medieval church of St Stephen" was Charles Heyer, Emilia and Robert's good friend and neighbour, who was simply thrilled to be a part, be it ever so tiny, of the project. "The money is very welcome for the upkeep[13] of the church," he had told Emilia, "and to make Mary Bennet a vicar is a splendid idea. I hope that it will be a bit of promotion[14] for St Stephen itself." For Charles, the only fly in the ointment[15] was that he had not even managed to grab a walk-on part[16], to say nothing of the role of the clergyman[17] in the adaptation of Jane Austen's book. "I'd *love* to play Mr Collins," he had sighed comically, "but they've set their minds on someone else, it seems."

Other filming locations, the *East Yorkshire News* said, were to be some rather grand houses nearby. A modern house was to be the equivalent of Jane Austen's Netherfield (the manor[18] where, if Emilia remembered correctly, Mr Darcy was a guest of friendly Mr Bingley and his snobbish sisters), and Rosedale Hall, a beautiful Jacobean[19] country house with magnificent gardens (and well-known to Emilia), would be Mr Darcy's Pemberley estate[20].

There will be plenty to talk about this evening, Emilia thought. She and Robert were having friends to dinner. Emilia was especially looking forward to seeing her friend Alix Hill, who worked as a research psychiatrist in a London hospital, but was in St Stephen on a regular basis – the main reason being her boyfriend, Detective Chief Inspector[21] David Rowe of the St Stephen police. Recently, David had had his hands full with the inquiry into the murder of a teenage girl, and from the intense media coverage[22] Emilia gathered[23] that it had been a difficult case to solve. As a private investigator[24] she had worked with David before, and had even got to know him when they were both involved in the same case. Also present would be Fiona Frommer and Charles Heyer, who was a very good cook and an aficionado[25] of detective stories and who, Emilia thought, was bound to have lots of information about the actors descending[26] on St Stephen …

---

12 passer-by: Passant  13 upkeep: Erhalt  14 promotion: Werbung  15 fly in the ointment: Haar in der Suppe  16 walk-on part: Statistenrolle  17 clergyman: Geistlicher  18 manor: Herrenhaus  19 Jacobean: aus der Zeit James' I. (1603–1625)  20 estate: Anwesen  21 Detective Chief Inspector (DCI): Rang bei der brit. Kriminalpolizei  22 media coverage: Medienberichterstattung  23 to gather: (hier) sich denken  24 private investigator: Privatdetektiv(in)  25 aficionado: Liebhaber, Fan  26 to descend on s.o./s.th.: über etw./jmd. herfallen

## Exercise 1

### Film and literature terms

Group the words a to l into threes. Find a term[27] that fits[28] the three words in each group.

*a) documentary – b) production/filming – c) leading role – d) newspaper article – e) novel – f) period film – g) poem – h) postproduction – i) preproduction – j) soap opera – k) supporting role – l) walk-on part*

When first Charles and then Alix arrived there was still plenty to do in the kitchen, not that anybody minded. Everybody lent a hand[29]. "David sends his apologies for being late," Alix explained. "He hopes to be around in an hour or so, something came up at the police station. We're not to delay dinner."

"I had hoped that he would have time to breathe, this nasty murder case being over," Emilia said. "He's still extremely busy. He hasn't had a day off[30] for weeks," Alix tried to sound unemotional, but Emilia thought that she found the situation trying. David's job as a policeman did not do their long-distance relationship[31] any good.

Shortly afterwards, Fiona arrived, and they began eating dinner. The conversation centered, of course, on the filming. "I remember reading *Pride and Prejudice* at school," Alix said. "Wasn't it about a family with three daughters, around 1800, all looking for husbands?" "It was five daughters, and most of the looking for husbands was done by their mother. Didn't you see the film?" Charles asked in an unbelieving voice, "or I should say films, there are several!" "They passed me by[32], I'm afraid," Alix said, "but I remember a Mr Darcy and a Mr Bingley, who got married to two of the daughters. Let me see if I remember their names …"

## Exercise 2

### Jane Austen's *Pride and Prejudice*

Have you read *Pride and Prejudice*? If not, read the plot summary at the end of this book. Note the names of the five Bennet sisters. Who are three of them married to at the end of the novel?

---

27 term: Begriff  28 to fit s.th.: zu etw. passen  29 to lend a hand: mithelfen  30 day off: freier Tag  31 long-distance relationship: Fernbeziehung  32 to pass s.o. by: jmd. entgehen

"I wonder what they're doing to bring the plot up to date," Fiona said. "It has been tried before, but with James Riddell as director[33] I'm kind of expecting something else, something special." "They're being rather tight-lipped[34] about all that," Charles replied. "The film company says it's an intelligent take on contemporary relationships, much as Jane Austen's novel was in her time, I'd say. Elizabeth Bennet is a gallery owner, Jane Bennet a doctor and Mary a vicar. Charles Bingley became rich by doing something with computers, I think, and William Darcy is a famous sculptor. Of course the names of the actors and their roles have been mentioned in the press releases[35]. It's an interesting cast[36]." "Yes, imagine Ivor Byrnes coming into the gallery. He's quite a catch[37] – and really handsome!" Fiona laughed.

"He's a wonderful actor," Robert said, "but I wouldn't have thought a light-hearted Jane Austen adaptation quite his style. The films he has done have all been rather ambitious." "It seems that he has worked with James Riddell before," Fiona remarked. "Maybe he did not want to become too fixed in a specific kind of role," Alix suggested. "And isn't it every actor's dream to play Mr Darcy?" Emilia asked. "I think it's a good idea to cast[38] someone like Byrnes as Darcy, who is always so very serious, but also, well, seriously good-looking."

"That also goes for[39] his Elizabeth Bennet," Charles said, "Nora Palliser is a real hot chick[40]." "Well, that's the expression I heard," he defended himself, when everyone looked at him. "And what else did you hear?" Emilia asked. "She had a good role in *The Lonely Hearts Hotel*," Charles explained. "The soap opera?" "Yes, she was very much praised for her acting, even if *Lonely Hearts Hotel* was not exactly quality TV[41]," Charles replied. "By the way, according to the press releases, there are to be some 'soap opera moments' in the *Bennet Sisters*, but at the same time it's said to be something completely different. And there won't be nearly as many episodes as in a soap opera. The first season[42] will have six episodes[43], which will be shown weekly." "So it's only semi-soapy[44]," Fiona suggested and everyone laughed.

"It's an interesting pairing," Robert mused, "Ivor Byrnes and Nora Palliser. I mean, in Jane Austen there was a notable difference in station[45] between Darcy and Elizabeth, which might be difficult to reproduce

---

33 director: Regisseur  34 tight-lipped: verschlossen  35 press release: Presseerklärung  36 cast: Besetzung  37 catch: Fang  38 to cast s.o.: jmd. eine Rolle geben  39 to go for: (hier) gelten  40 hot chick (ugs.): steiler Zahn  41 quality TV: anspruchsvolles Fernsehen  42 first season: erste Staffel  43 episode: Folge  44 semi-soapy: (etwa) nur halb wie eine Soap Opera (soapy: seifig)  45 station: (sozialer) Stand

nowadays. It's an interesting idea to pair a highbrow[46] actor with a soap opera star."

"You're right," Charles agreed. "Especially when you consider that for Nora Palliser being part of a soap opera cast was a step up the ladder[47], if you understand what I mean."

Emilia knew that Charles had eclectic[48] interests, but she did wonder where he had this piece of information from. "How do you know all of this, Charles?" she inquired.

"You know, often it's my job to simply listen …," Charles said innocently, "and the filming was the number one topic[49] at the last meeting of the Women's Institute[50]." He sighed theatrically. "You don't know how I suffered!" Emilia only raised an eyebrow at him.

Exercise 3

### Typical characters in stories

Have another look at the plot of Jane Austen's *Pride and Prejudice*. Who is/are

*1. the hero – 2. the heroine – 3. the hero's antagonist – 4. the villain – 5. (the) protagonist(s) – 6. someone's love interest – 7. (a) supporting character(s)?*

*a) Elizabeth Bennet – b) Jane Bennet – c) Mr Bingley – d) Mr Collins – e) Mr Darcy – f) Mr Wickham*

The bell rang and Emilia got up to open the door. "I'm sorry for being so dreadfully late," David Rowe said when she gave him a quick hug[51]. "That's all right, we all know that you've been up to your ears in work," she replied, noticing that he was looking very tired indeed. "Yes," he agreed, "and I'd rather talk about something else this evening." "Don't worry," Emilia laughed, "we've been getting excited about the TV series they're filming. Have you heard about the *Pride and Prejudice* adaptation, the *Lives and Loves of the Bennet Sisters*? Charles is regaling[52] us with tidbits[53] of information he claims he picked up from the WI women."

---

46 highbrow: (betont) intellektuell 47 step up the ladder: Schritt nach vorne/oben 48 eclectic: sehr unterschiedlich 49 topic: (Gesprächs-)Thema 50 Women's Institute (WI): brit., bes. auf dem Land aktive Frauenorganisation (Ziel ist u. a. die Weiterbildung von Frauen) 51 hug: Umarmung 52 to regale: erfreuen, ergötzen 53 tidbit: Leckerbissen, Pikanterie

They entered the room where the others were sitting. David smiled. "I've picked up some information myself," he answered Emilia's question. "A number of CID[54] colleagues, Maud Johnstone for example, are great fans of Ivor Byrnes, but another actor, I forget his name, is less popular. He played a corrupt policeman in some crime series." David sat down next to Alix on the sofa. "I do hope that there are no detectives or crime victims in Jane Austen or this new series." "We don't know yet," Fiona said, "but I think it is safe to assume that there are not."

"Have you read the book, David?" Emilia wanted to know. "Jane Austen? Nah …," David raised his hands, "I don't think that …" "You don't think it manly enough?" Alix asked, pretending to be very serious indeed. "Well, I do not know any men who've read it …," David defended himself. "You know at least two," Charles said, "I've read it, and I think that Robert has as well." "Oh, several times," Robert simply said. "It's great literature, and it was written at the time I'm interested in." "All right," David replied, admitting defeat[55], "but for a policeman, it's not exactly compulsory reading[56]." "Especially for a policeman, a bit of non-compulsory or even escapist[57] reading might be just the thing[58]," Alix said lightly. "Point taken[59]," David replied, smiling at her.

### Exercise 4

### Idioms: Reading and writing

Idioms (Redewendungen) are frequently used in spoken language. Often, the (figurative[60]) meaning of idioms differs from the (literal[61]) meaning of the words constituting them.

Find the German equivalents for the following idioms:

*1. by every trick in the book – 2. by the book – 3. don't judge a book by its cover – 4. that's nothing to write home about – 5. to be written all over one's face – 6. to drop s.o. a line – 7. to put a pen to paper – 8. to take a page out of s.o.'s book – 9. to take s.th. as read – 10. to throw the book at s.o. – 11. written in stone*

---

54 CID (Criminal Investigation Department): die brit. Kriminalpolizei  55 to admit defeat: eine Niederlage eingestehen  56 compulsory reading: Pflichtlektüre  57 escapist: der Realität entfliehend  58 just the thing (ugs.): genau das Richtige  59 point taken: (etwa) ich sehe es ein  60 figurative meaning: übertragene Bedeutung  61 literal meaning: wörtliche Bedeutung

*a) damit lässt sich kein Eindruck schinden – b) fest von etw. ausgehen –
c) genau nach Vorschrift – d) in Stein gemeißelt – e) ins Gesicht geschrieben –
f) jmd. so streng wie möglich bestrafen – g) jmd. (kurz) schreiben –
h) nach allen Regeln der Kunst – i) sich von jmd. eine Scheibe abschneiden –
j) ziehe keine voreiligen Schlüsse – k) zur Feder greifen*

Filming began on Monday. During breakfast Emilia barely dissuaded[62] Robert from accompanying her to the gallery, promising faithfully not to let anything happen to the paintings. The film crew was due at nine, and a first meeting with the actors (who had been rehearsing[63] until the week before) was scheduled[64] for the afternoon.

The gallery was in an attractive Georgian terraced house[65] in the centre of St Stephen. When Robert and Stella had bought the property a number of years ago, it had been in a dreadful state and they had knocked[66] several rooms at the front into one big gallery space. They had, however, been able to keep the original entrance door with its fanlight[67] and the bay window[68], which had been lovingly restored. Inside, a wooden floor of reclaimed timber[69] contrasted beautifully with the walls, which, only the year before, had been painted sage[70] green.

Emilia was there early and was interested to see that the gallery space had undergone some transformation. The pictures Robert had painstakingly acquired and hoped to sell were still there (as stipulated in the contract), but in one corner there was a small and very chic reception and office area and with wiring[71], lighting and other equipment the whole room had obviously been kitted out for the filming. Before Emilia was able to have a good look around, however, another person arrived, a woman of about her own age. She was pleasant-looking, quite small and had a shock[72] of almost black shoulder-length hair. "Hi, I'm Kathleen Cochrane, the second assistant director[73]," she introduced herself. "Emilia Ramsay," Emilia replied. "Pleased to meet you."

---

62 to dissuade: abbringen  63 to rehearse: proben  64 scheduled: (zeitlich) angesetzt  65 Georgian terraced house: Haus in einer Häuserzeile aus dem 18./frühen 19. Jhd.  66 to knock into: zusammenlegen  67 fanlight: fächerförmiges Oberlicht einer Tür  68 bay window: Erkerfenster  69 reclaimed timber: recycelte Holzdielen  70 sage: Salbei  71 wiring: Verkabelung  72 shock: (hier) Schopf  73 assistant director (AD): Regieassistent

## Exercise 5

### Introducing oneself

There are a number of ways to introduce oneself at the beginning of a conversation. Which of the following are more formal, which are not?

1. *Allow me to introduce myself. My name is …*
2. *Hi, I'm Kathy.*
3. *My name is Emilia Ramsay.*
4. *Good afternoon, I'm Kathleen Cochrane.*
5. *May I introduce myself? I'm Robert Rutherford.*
6. *Hello, I'm Kathleen, Kathleen Cochrane, but please call me Kathy.*

---

"I was told that you would be present," Kathleen said, "but you know that it's not really necessary? We'll take good care of everything, as I've told the owners." Emilia explained about the pictures, that they should not be exposed to too much light and that Mr Rutherford and Ms Lloyd would prefer if someone they knew was present.

"Yes, it's part of the contract," Kathleen remembered, "I only wanted to say that there is no need to worry." "I am sure there isn't," Emilia replied, "and I'll mainly be in the back of the gallery. I won't be getting under your feet[74] much." She intended to do her own work in Robert's office, which was not being used by the film company. "Oh, I'm sure everything will work out fine," Kathleen smiled.

"What is it exactly that you do?" Emilia wanted to know. "I'm responsible for much of the day-to-day operation," Kathleen explained, "a kind of backstage[75] manager cum[76] general dogsbody[77]." She grinned. "One of my tasks is to prepare the daily call sheets[78] and to see that the actors are in the right place at the right time. You'll see me bossing[79] them around!" "Since you're here," she added, "I'll introduce you to everybody. You might like to get a glimpse of what is going on – I need not remind you that another part of the contract is that no details about anything happening during the

---

74 to get under one's feet (ugs.): jmd. vor den Füßen herumlaufen  75 backstage: hinter den Kulissen
76 cum: in Verbindung mit  77 general dogsbody: Mädchen für alles  78 call sheet: Ablaufplan eines Drehtags  79 to boss s.o. around: jmd. herumkommandieren

filming are to become public?" Emilia promised to be discreet – making a mental note[80] to impress[81] on Charles that anything she told him was not to go any further!

Shortly afterwards, lots of people arrived. Besides Kathleen Cochrane, who was called Kathy by everyone, there was Christopher Cox, the first assistant director, location manager Emma Gill, two camera operators, the gaffer (or chief lighting technician) Paolo Costa, who Emilia briefly talked to about the pictures, and a number of other crew members, whose jobs Emilia wasn't told. Quickly and expertly they made the finishing touches[82] to adapt the gallery space to the purposes[83] of the filming. They were still waiting for director James Riddell.

**Exercise 6**

### Film professions

Match the film professions with their job descriptions.

*1. actor – 2. assistant director – 3. camera operator – 4. director – 5. gaffer – 6. location manager*

a) *organises things on set, checks progress against production schedule, prepares call sheets, puts actors through make-up and wardrobe*

b) *physically operates a camera and has some say in how to use it to achieve the aims of the director*

c) *plans and realises the lighting of a film production*

d) *plays a character in a film or stage production*

e) *responsible for the artistic goals of a film, directs the actors and the film crew to reach them*

f) *secures a film's locations and coordinates lots of things related to them*

In the afternoon, the gallery space really began to fill. The aim of the meeting was to make the actors familiar with the new surroundings before the filming proper[84] began. It would mainly be done in the big gallery space.

80 to make a mental note: sich merken  81 to impress on s.o.: jmd. einschärfen  82 to make the finishing touches: letzte Hand anlegen  83 purpose: Zweck  84 filming proper: die eigentlichen Filmaufnahmen

"The camera crew and all the technicians will be over there," Emma Gill explained to Emilia. She pointed to the back part of the room. "And the actors will mainly be where you see Ivor standing, or near." Emilia looked at Ivor Byrnes, who had arrived only minutes before and had not yet taken off his coat. A number of people came up to him, greeting him and talking to him, but his answers seemed to be, Emilia thought, a bit economical. Still, he was a very good-looking man, tall and dark-haired and with an interesting face. "He'll make a splendid Mr Darcy, don't you think?" Emma asked her. "He has presence," Emilia agreed, "and even his personality might be a bit like Mr Darcy's." "You mean that he appears to be somewhat aloof[85]?" Emma had evidently read her thoughts. "He is an important actor," she continued, "he comes from an acting family, went to RADA[86] and acted in a number of very good films, but continued taking part in stage productions[87] as well. A few years ago, James Riddell saw him as Hamlet in Stratford[88] and was impressed. He offered him the lead[89] in *Night Thoughts*, for which Ivor got his BAFTA." "That was pretty serious stuff," Emilia remembered, "it's interesting that now they're doing a Jane Austen adaptation together." Emma smiled. "James does not want to be pigeonholed[90]," she said, "and Ivor might have come to the conclusion that he doesn't either."

### Exercise 7

### Literary genres

Connect each literary genre with an appropriate title (some of the listed titles exist, some do not).

| | |
|---|---|
| *biography* | *Hamlet* |
| *detective story* | *Jane Austen: A Life* |
| *novel* | *Murder at Pemberley* |
| *play* | *Voyage to Planet Austen* |
| *science fiction* | *Yorkshire and the North York Moors* |
| *travel guide* | *Pride and Prejudice* |

---

[85] aloof: distanziert  [86] RADA: Royal Academy of Dramatic Art  [87] stage production: Bühnenproduktion
[88] Stratford: Stratford-upon-Avon, der Sitz der Royal Shakespeare Company  [89] lead: Hauptrolle
[90] to pigeonhole: in eine Schublade stecken

Moments later, Emilia had a first glimpse of the leading man[91] and the leading lady together. Nora Palliser, who Emilia had exchanged a few friendly words with earlier, came up to Ivor Byrnes and they spoke to each other. Charles was right, Emilia thought, she is really quite something. Nora was not conventionally beautiful, but with her curvy figure, strawberry blond hair (which reminded Emilia of the colour of Alix's hair, but Alix was willowy[92] and taller than Nora) and open expression, Emilia could understand that many found her irresistible – there even was a smile on Ivor Byrnes's face when Nora spoke to him!

Now Christopher Cox, the first AD, was standing next to Emilia. An hour ago, he had taken pains[93] to explain a lot to her, for which she was grateful, and she felt that, with him and Kathy Cochrane, Robert's gallery was in good hands. "What do you think?" Christopher asked non-committally[94], but there was a twinkle in his eyes. "Oh," Emilia was surprised at his question, but then she understood. "I think that as Darcy and Elizabeth, they'll do[95]," she said.

"Do you know who's who yet?" Christopher asked her. "No, not yet," Emilia replied. "Kathy introduced me to Mr Bingley, I mean to Nicholas Trent, but who are the lady and the man standing next to him?" She pointed to a corner, where Nicholas Trent – who with his light brown curls and almost constant smile Emilia imagined to be a very apt choice[96] for happy-go-lucky[97] Charles Bingley – stood with a tall, but fragile looking woman and a man with very short hair and a crooked[98] nose, which made him oddly[99] attractive. "That's Jessica Sleightholme," said Christopher. "She is not quite as serene[100] as she's supposed to be as Jane Bennet. She's especially grumpy[101] in the mornings – I thought I ought to let you know … – Next to her is Alan Gibson, who's been cast as Andrew Fitzwilliam. From what I've seen of him, he seems a nice chap."

James Riddell had come into the middle of the room and was asking for everybody's attention. The director gave a short speech, welcoming all those present. "This is our first day on location," he said. "Make yourself familiar[102] with the surroundings and try to keep in mind what we've spoken about during rehearsals. We'll be entering the production phase tomorrow, and over the next weeks there will be an awful lot of work to do. We'll be done here in about three weeks. Then there will a few days' break,

---

91 leading man/lady: Hauptdarsteller/in  92 willowy: gertenschlank  93 to take pains: sich Mühe geben  94 non-committally: neutral, unverbindlich  95 they'll do: (etwa) das wird mit ihnen schon klappen  96 apt choice: gute (passende) Wahl  97 happy-go-lucky: unbeschwert  98 crooked: schief  99 odd: seltsam, eigentümlich  100 serene: heiter, gelassen  101 grumpy: schlecht gelaunt  102 familiar: vertraut

which will be well-deserved[103] by you all, and afterwards we'll continue with the Pemberley scenes. We're trying to keep strictly to our production schedule, which, as always, is tight and terribly complicated. Any questions concerning this schedule and many other questions should be sorted out[104] with assistant directors Kathy and Christopher, especially the question," James lowered his voice dramatically, "of when I want you here."

### Exercise 8

#### Introducing others

Which of the following four sentences have the same meaning? Find the differences between the sentences in each pair (in terms of their degree of formality and their wording).

1. *Mr Byrnes, may I present Kathleen Cochrane?*

2. *James, this is Nora. Nora, James.*

3. *Ivor, say hello to Kathy.*

4. *Mr Riddell, I'd like you to meet Nora Palliser. Nora, this is James Riddell.*

He then gave a few pointers[105] on how he intended to use the gallery space and left everyone to their tasks. Emilia went to Robert's office to write a number of e-mails. She was looking forward to her three weeks in the gallery – they were going to be interesting, and both the actors and the production crew were professional and, on the whole[106], friendly.

Later, she went to the small kitchen where the caterers had left a supply of tea, coffee, cake and sandwiches. Before she could enter the room, however, she heard voices, an unbelieving voice, which was Kathy's, and another one, which she recognised as Ivor Byrnes's. Emilia was tempted to listen, but it really wasn't her business. "I'm not here as a private investigator," she reminded herself.

---

103 well-deserved: wohlverdient  104 to sort out a question: eine Frage klären  105 pointer: Hinweis
106 on the whole: im Großen und Ganzen

## Exercise 9

**Things to say or ask when introducing oneself**

Complete the following:

1. _____. – The pleasure is all mine.

2. _____, it's a pleasure to finally meet you.

3. I didn't introduce myself. My name is Emilia Ramsay.
   _____?

4. How do you do? – _____?

by inserting one of these sentences:

a) I've heard so much about you

b) How do you do

c) What's your name

d) I'm delighted to finally meet you


When she came back a short time later, Kathy was still in the kitchen, blue eyes blazing[107]. "Is anything the matter?" Emilia asked. "Oh, it's a minor thing to some people," Kathy said. "Ivor has persuaded Nicholas Trent and Jessica Sleightholme not to rough it[108] in the humble[109] four-star hotel that's been booked for the actors and is separated by only a few streets from the gallery. They've taken a luxury holiday let[110], a house that Ivor says is not too far off and private, so I'm sure it's in the middle of nowhere. Now there will be plenty of things for me to reorganise."

"I'm sorry to hear that," Emilia commiserated[111], but then she had to laugh. "So they've really got into the spirit of things[112]," she said, "they've rented their very own Netherfield!" Kathy looked at her. "Their own Netherfield," she repeated, a grin spreading over her face, "you can be sure that I'll be making use of that expression!"

---

107 to blaze: funkeln  108 to rough it (ugs.): ohne jeden Komfort leben  109 humble: bescheiden  110 holiday let: Ferienhaus  111 to commiserate: bedauern  112 to get into the spirit of things: sich für etw. begeistern, sich einer Sache verschreiben

### Exercise 10

Translate

Words and phrases from this chapter might help you.

1. *Ich freue mich sehr, Sie kennenzulernen. Ich habe viel von Ihnen gehört.*

2. *Wir haben Freunde zum Abendessen. Ich freue mich darauf, sie wiederzusehen.*

3. *Das ist eine hervorragende Idee, doch würde ich lieber über etwas anderes reden.*

# Chapter 2

Things quickly settled in a routine. Over the next few days, Emilia divided her time in the gallery between watching the filming – which was mainly interesting but sometimes tedious[1] – and doing her own work in Robert's office – which, being Internet research and writing reports, was mainly tedious. So it was a welcome diversion[2] when some of the actors dropped in[3]. Despite Kathy's meticulous[4] organisation they often had to wait for short periods until they were called for filming.

"They're repeating it for the umpteenth time[5]," Leo Sandys had come into the room, "James wants more subtle rivalry between Elizabeth and Caroline Bingley, and you can tell that Jean and Nora are fed up." Jean Whyte was the actress playing snobbish Caroline Bingley, but actually a very likeable person – like Leo, who had been cast as George Wickham, the villain[6] of both *Pride and Prejudice* and the *Bennet Sisters*, and, Emilia suspected, would much have preferred to be nice Mr Bingley.

"He's needling[7] them until everything they say comes out with a waspish[8] undertone," Alan Gibson stated. He had appropriated[9] the armchair next to Robert's bookcase and was pretending to read a book ("If I'm disturbing you, simply ask me to bugger off[10]," he had told Emilia). Alan's was the role of Andrew Fitzwilliam, Darcy's cousin. It was not large, but more important than in the book – in the new adaptation he was to be a real rival for Elizabeth Bennet's affections[11].

"Anyone up for a walk?" Jessica Sleightholme looked into the room. "The weather is quite nice and they will be at it for hours." "Thanks, but I'll pass[12]. I'd rather not be chased by the press again," Leo replied. Jessica came into the room as well. "I forgot," she sighed.

"This waiting is getting on my nerves," she said a few minutes later, during which everyone had tried to read or work. "I'd elope[13] with you to Italy any time, my dear Jessica," Alan said gallantly. "Don't you dare," Nora Palliser had suddenly appeared, "not without me!" "So you're finished," Leo said. "At last," Nora leaned against the wall, as if desperately needing support. "So what about Italy?" she asked. "If we hurry up," Alan

---

1 tedious: langweilig  2 diversion: Ablenkung  3 to drop in: vorbeischauen  4 meticulous: sehr genau  5 for the umpteenth time: zum zigsten Mal  6 villain: Schurke  7 to needle s.o.: jmd. piesacken  8 waspish: giftig, reizbar  9 to appropriate: in Beschlag nehmen  10 to bugger off (ugs.): abhauen, verduften  11 affections: Gefühle  12 I'll pass: nein danke  13 to elope: durchbrennen

said, getting up and offering Nora his arm, "we might make it for dinner in Rome. Sorry Jessica, darling …" Everyone laughed.

"Here you are – disturbing Ms Ramsay," said Ivor Byrnes, whom nobody had seen entering. "There's a perfectly good room for us to wait in next door. Alan and Nora, James wants us."

### Exercise 11

Who's who?

Which person has which function or plays which role in *The Lives and Loves of the Bennet Sisters*?

Persons: *1. Alan Gibson – 2. Christopher Cox – 3. Emma Gill – 4. Ivor Byrnes – 5. James Riddell – 6. Jean Whyte – 7. Jessica Sleightholme – 8. Kathleen Cochrane – 9. Leo Sandys – 10. Nicholas Trent – 11. Nora Palliser*

Functions or roles: *a) Andrew Fitzwilliam – b) Caroline Bingley – c) Charles Bingley – d) director – e) Elizabeth Bennet – f) first assistant director – g) George Wickham – h) Jane Bennet – i) location manager – j) second assistant director – k) William Darcy*

The room emptied quickly after that. Privately, Emilia (who had been rereading *Pride and Prejudice*) sometimes amused herself by comparing the actors to the characters they played – realising, of course, that she did not know them very well. But there were some interesting similarities. A person she couldn't quite make up her mind about was Ivor. From what Emilia could tell, he was a wonderful and extremely professional actor, who, on set, was perfectly civil, at times even friendly. But the private Ivor Byrnes seemed to be another matter. Sometimes he was a bit arrogant, otherwise he did not say very much. Was he too proud to mingle[14] with everyone or was he simply shy? Or was he a very private person? He seemed to be less stiff in his interactions with Nora Palliser, Emilia observed, who had got into the habit of teasing[15] him. Did Nora want to draw him out of his shell[16] or did she simply think that even Ivor should be made to contribute

---

14 to mingle: sich unter die Leute mischen  15 to tease: necken  16 to draw s.o. out of his shell: jmd. aus der Reserve locken

his share[17] to a general conversation? Or was there a genuine[18] attraction between the two?

Nora Palliser made an enchanting[19] Elizabeth Bennet and as a person she was no less charming. She had a very expressive face, which made whoever she was talking to feel that she was truly interested. Emilia could tell that she was ambitious, but what made her like her was the fact that Nora seemed to be a tiny bit insecure about playing this important role in a prestigious production.

**Exercise 12**

### Beginning a conversation

Emilia gets to know everyone on set by talking to them. She breaks the ice by asking questions typical for initiating a conversation. Have a look at the answers and formulate questions Emilia could ask.

1. _____ – I've known Nicholas for two years, but it's the first time that I have worked with the other actors.

2. _____
 – I met James at the premiere of the last film I played a part in.

3. _____
 – It is. I love this kind of autumn weather – cold, but sunny.

4. _____ – I've never been to the Yorkshire countryside, but last year I spent a few days in York.

5. My name is Emilia. _____
 – Oh, I did not introduce myself. I'm Leo Sandys.

6. _____ – It's really comfortable. I've got a big double bed in my room and my own bathroom.

Another person Emilia got to know better, and became quite friendly with, was Kathy Cochrane. The second AD could always be seen with a clipboard[20] and a pen, making notes and ticking off[21] things on a list, or making

---

17 share: Anteil  18 genuine: wirklich  19 enchanting: bezaubernd  20 clipboard: Klemmbrett  21 to tick off: abhaken

phone calls on her mobile. "You have to ask Kathy," or "Kathy will tell you what to do," were sentences often heard. "She bosses us all around," James Riddell said. Mostly, this was done gently, but Kathy could become quite determined. "I am not your mother," she told Ivor, who had arrived late for a make-up call[22]. "I should very much hope not," Ivor replied in a decisive tone.

Kathy and Emilia often spent a few minutes together (until Kathy had to rush off), exchanging humorous remarks about what was going on. Kathy even found out that Emilia was a private investigator – the others hadn't bothered to ask and probably thought that she worked in Robert and Stella's gallery. Emilia, who was discreet about her job, saw no reason to enlighten[23] them that she was in another line of work altogether.

Kathy was discreet about the actors and her colleagues, but there were some details she let slip to Emilia. Jessica Sleightholme sometimes required special treatment, and Ivor Byrnes was obviously exasperating[24] Kathy by doing things and only telling her about it afterwards. "I am not in the business of reading his mind," she said. "Why can't the man communicate like anyone else?" Christopher Cox had bought quite a nice flat in London, and Alan Gibson had obviously gone through a hard time and was grateful for getting the role of Andrew Fitzwilliam. Nora Palliser, at the beginning of the filming, had felt a bit out of her depth[25] and had had a good cry on Kathy's shoulder. She was surer of herself now, Kathy was pleased to say.

### Exercise 13

#### Talking about people

Find the phrases and idioms used for someone who is

*1. a lively young man (with lots of girlfriends) – 2. boring – 3. emotionally supportive – 4. not very intelligent – 5. often not telling the truth – 6. very amusing – 7. very nice – 8. your friend for as long as you don't have any problems*

*a) a born entertainer – b) a compulsive liar – c) a crashing bore – d) a fair-weather friend – e) a shoulder to cry on – f) as nice as they come – g) not the sharpest tool in the box – h) quite a lad*

22 make-up call: Termin für die Maske  23 to enlighten s.o.: jmd. aufklären  24 to exasperate: (ver)ärgern
25 out of one's depth: überfordert

"You must come," Nicholas Trent said to Emilia. "We've spent so much time in your office that I'd like to return the favour[26]."

Nicholas was inviting all the cast and crew to a party at the luxury holiday house that he, with Ivor and Jessica, had rented. He wanted to celebrate, the reason being that, James Riddell having other commitments, there was to be a week-long pause in the filming. The actors, however, could not immediately leave St Stephen for a holiday (and, Emilia thought, to catch up on much-needed sleep), because a press conference had been set for the first day of the break. Kathy had impressed on them that everybody had to be present. "We've had plenty of interest from the media," she had said. "The press office has managed to string them along[27] with the promise of a big 'meet the actors' session, and they expect you all to be there. Truth to tell, we've only been bothered a bit by journalists, and I'd very much like it to remain that way."

"I'd really like you to come," Nicholas insisted. "You've put up with us bored and bickering[28] and we can be so much nicer. Only yesterday Ivor said that we must have got on your nerves." "Ivor said that?" Emilia asked, a bit more sharply than she had intended, but then she tempered[29] her tone. "As a matter of fact, you didn't. If you had, I'd have found a way of telling you," she said, privately thinking that Ivor had been rather patronising[30]. "What I was doing was a bit tedious, so it was actually nice to have someone to talk to." "So you'll come?" Nicholas asked, looking like an eager little boy. "And why don't you bring a friend or two? The place Ivor found us is big enough." "Of course I will," Emilia promised. "And I might take you up on your offer to bring a friend." She knew that Robert would be busy that evening, but a party with the actors might be just the thing for Charles.

Exercise 14

### Frequently used phrases and idioms

Have a look at this chapter so far and find the phrases for:

*1. Das tue ich lieber nicht. – 2. genau das Richtige – 3. sich (mit etwas Nettem) revanchieren – 4. sich etw. zur Gewohnheit werden lassen – 5. sich über jmd. eine Meinung bilden – 6. sich überfordert fühlen – 7. Wage es bloß nicht!*

---

[26] to return a favour: sich revanchieren  [27] to string s.o. along: jmd. hinhalten  [28] to bicker: sich kabbeln
[29] to temper: mäßigen  [30] patronising: herablassend

When Emilia got out of her car at the venue[31] of the party near the village of Moreton-le-Moor – a twenty-minute drive from St Stephen plus a good five minutes on a single-track road[32] – the first thing she did was admire her surroundings. It being the end of November, the sun had set hours ago, but in the moonlight she could see a large and attractive limestone[33] farmhouse, all the windows of which were lighted. Through the French windows[34] of the modern extension[35] Emilia could catch a glimpse of the interior, which was simply, but very tastefully and not inexpensively done. And she could see that there were plenty of people – Nicholas had obviously invited everybody, despite his housemates trying to keep things simple, as Jessica had put it.

"That's quite a holiday pad[36]," Charles had got out of the car as well, "I wonder how much it costs to rent it." "It's certainly out of my price range, even now in the low season[37]," Emilia replied. They went into the house, where the large hall, the even larger living room and the big kitchen were filled with guests.

"There you are," Nicholas Trent had seen them coming in, "I hope that you found it alright. We're quite secluded, as you see." "With your directions we were fine," Emilia replied and introduced Charles. "So you're the vicar of the church some of us will be filming at soon! That's splendid!" Nicholas was thrilled to meet Charles. "I have to introduce you to Dan and Alison. You know that Alison Reid is vicar Mary Bennet and that Dan Parker is her curate[38] Mr Collins? Maybe you can give them a few pointers[39]." Charles replied that he had heard of both actors and would, of course, be absolutely delighted to talk about his profession. Nicholas did not have to be told twice and, together with Charles, went to look for Dan and Alison. And so Emilia, glass in hand, found herself alone near the passage to the kitchen.

After the intense work of the last weeks, the actors were really going to let their hair down[40], she realised. Nicholas had hired the caterers who also provided the food on set, so there was plenty to eat and drink, and already lots of empty beer and open wine bottles. Soft music was coming from a sound system and Alan Gibson and first AD Christopher Cox were shifting the big sofas near the fireplace to make room for dancing. Someone turned up the volume of the music and suddenly the room was even fuller and people began to dance.

---

31 venue: (Veranstaltungs-)Ort  32 single-track road: einspurige Fahrbahn  33 limestone: Kalkstein  34 French window: Bodenfenster  35 extension: Anbau  36 pad (ugs.): Bude  37 low season: Nebensaison  38 curate: (etwa) Hilfspfarrer  39 pointer: Hinweis  40 to let one's hair down (ugs.): sich sehr ungezwungen benehmen

## Exercise 15

### Other filmmaking professions

Many members of the film crew are present at the party. Find the job descriptions for their professions.

*1. boom operator – 2. director of audiography – 3. director of photography – 4. make-up artist – 5. props master – 6. script supervisor – 7. unit production manager*

*a) applies make-up to the actors' faces and sometimes even changes their appearance – b) makes sure that all the parts of the script are filmed, notes every detail of a scene to ensure continuity from shot to shot – c) manages a film production and sees that it does not exceed its budget – d) manages the camera operators and lighting crew – e) responsible for placing the microphone (on a long boom pole[41]) in the right places – f) sources and manages the props[42] in a film – g) the head of the sound department of a film*

Emilia went into the kitchen, where things were quieter, but only just. "Emilia!" Kathy, who was standing with several of the actors, shouted and beckoned[43] her to come over. Emilia noted that Kathy looked different. Normally, she wore casual clothes and pinned up her hair, but now she was wearing it loose and had donned[44] a silky blue dress that went very well with her blue eyes. "Doesn't she look stunning," Leo said to Emilia, complimenting her on her own dress as well. Leo, Emilia realised, was tipsy[45] already and the others weren't exactly sober. "Very charming, Mr Wickham," Kathy said, which led Leo to talk about his role and his plans to change it as much as James Riddell would allow – it was his intention to bring to light the hitherto[46] undiscovered depths of George Wickham! This was the start of an animated[47], funny and partly downright[48] silly discussion about how much change to Jane Austen's characters the new series could get away with[49]. "We've done that quite a lot already," Jean Whyte said, "it's supposed to be realistic, after all!" "What is your impression?" she asked Emilia.

Emilia had to admit that she had only caught snippets[50] of the plot. Only a certain amount of scenes were filmed in the gallery, and what was

---

41 boom pole: Tonangel (langer Stab für ein Mikrofon)  42 props: Requisiten  43 to beckon to s.o.: jmd. herbeibeiwinken  44 to don: anziehen, anlegen  45 tipsy: beschwipst  46 hitherto: bis jetzt  47 animated: lebhaft  48 downright: regelrecht  49 to get away with s.th.: mit etw. davonkommen  50 snippet: Bruchstück

also confusing was that the sequence of the scenes filmed did not correspond to the sequence in the final series. "But having read *Pride and Prejudice* again," she laughed, "I've discovered some modernisations that I quite like." "Like making Darcy an important sculptor?" Nora asked, who next to Kathy was sitting on the kitchen counter. "Don't you think it a bit sexist, him being a famous artist and Elizabeth a humble gallery owner? What would you say, Ivor?"

Ivor Byrnes had arrived at their group a couple of minutes before, but had only listened and looked at Nora. "What we need," Ivor said, "is a reversal[51] of the sexes in *Pride and Prejudice*." Emilia had to concede[52] that this was a good point[53], but Ivor had given his reply so deadpan[54] that she did not know if there was any irony in it.

"But would the viewers like it? Their good opinion once lost, is lost forever," Nora, who seemed to know the book by heart, said. "That is *my* line," Ivor said, suddenly smiling.

The discussion continued in this vein[55], with Nora and Ivor bickering. "What we couldn't get away with is too much change in Elizabeth and Darcy," Kathy softly said to Emilia. "Look at them – aren't they just perfect?" Emilia could only agree.

### Exercise 16

#### Making small talk

Which of the following statements are true, which are false?

1. *Nobody is interested in small talk, so don't bother with it.*

2. *Small talk is important to break the ice and maybe to get into a more meaningful conversation later.*

3. *Controversial themes make small talk more interesting.*

4. *Dispensing with small talk and approaching the really important topics at once is often considered impolite.*

5. *Memorising a number of small talk topics might be useful for a party or the beginning of a business meeting.*

---

51 reversal: Umkehrung  52 to concede: zugeben  53 good point: gutes Argument  54 deadpan: trocken, mit ausdrucksloser Miene  55 in this vein: auf diese Art  56 to be engaged in s.th.: mit etw. beschäftigt sein  57 C of E (kurz für Church of England): die anglikanische Kirche  58 to crash (ugs.): pennen  59 to be taken aback: (unangenehm) überrascht sein

She went in search of Charles, whom she hadn't seen for some time. She needn't have worried – he was upstairs and happily engaged[56] in some kind of 'All you ever wanted to know about the C of E[57] and never dared to ask'-game with Dan Parker and Alison Reid. After mainly listening for some time, Emilia went back downstairs, where the kitchen was now much emptier because everyone was dancing. When she got herself another drink, Alan appeared next to her. "You have to drive," he said, pointing to her glass. "Yes," Emilia said. "Me too," Alan replied. "But," he added hopefully, "we could have a few glasses and then crash[58] in one of the empty bedrooms."

Emilia was a bit taken aback[59], not quite sure if Alan was propositioning[60] her. "We'd awake with a dreadful hangover," she said lightly and was happy that he seemed to take the hint. "You're probably right," Alan said good-naturedly, but with a hint of regret in his voice. "So may I have the next dance? There's not much room, you'll only have to shuffle your feet[61] a bit …"

Emila danced with Alan, but everybody was swapping dance partners, so she danced next with Leo, with some others and then with Nicholas. "It's a very nice party," she said. "Yes, everyone's relaxing a bit," Nicholas replied, "with the exception of Ivor." "But I saw him dancing," Emilia replied, "with Nora and then Kathy ended up with him." "Oh," Nicholas said. "He hasn't been too happy lately," he added, "so let's cut him some slack[62]." Emilia raised an inquiring eyebrow at him, but Nicholas did not say any more.

Some time later, Charles came looking for Emilia. "Pumpkin time[63]," he said regretfully. "It's after midnight, I've got a meeting with the archdeacon[64] tomorrow morning and I still have to prepare!"

### Exercise 17

### Small talk topics

Combine the phrases on the following page into sentences addressing typical small talk topics (someone's journey, the area you are in, your host or hostess, your immediate surroundings, children).

---

60 to proposition s.o.: jmd. einen (eindeutigen) Antrag machen  61 to shuffle one's feet: mit den Füßen scharren, (hier) ein wenig die Füße bewegen  62 to cut s.o. some slack (ugs.): jmd. gegenüber nachsichtig sein  63 pumpkin time: Zeit schlafen zu gehen (wenn sich Cinderellas Kutsche um Mitternacht in einen Kürbis [pumpkin] verwandelt)  64 archdeacon: Erzdiakon

*a lovely house. – any children? – did not have any trouble – Do you happen to know – Do you have – for quite some time. – How do you – how they have done the kitchen. – I have never been – I hope that you – I like – I think that – I've known him – if Nicholas owns it? – know Nicholas? – the landscape is simply beautiful. – This is – to find your way here. – to Yorkshire.*

Shortly after four in the morning, David Rowe was woken by the ringing of his mobile. "We've got a suspicious accident near Moreton," one of his colleagues, who was on night duty at the police station, said, "a man died. You'd better have a look." David cursed inwardly. "I'll be there as soon as possible," he said.

He arrived at the site of the accident thirty minutes later, a steep hill just out of Moreton, the upper part of which was crossed by a road. On the side of the decline[65] there was a lay-by[66], where he recognised the van of the crime scene team, an ambulance and the car of DS[67] Maud Johnstone. Someone had installed a lamp, and down the hillside David could see a car in the glare of further lights. Maud was standing a bit to the side with an elderly man and his elderly dog, which to David looked as if it would rather be at home asleep. He could relate[68] to that.

### Exercise 18

**Translate**

Phrases used in this chapter might help you.

1. *Wage es nicht, mich herumzukommandieren!*
2. *Er gewöhnte sich an, abends ein paar Gläser zu trinken.*
3. *Er hatte eine harte Zeit durchgemacht. Deshalb war die neue Wohnung genau das Richtige.*

Maud Johnstone made the introductions. "This is Detective Chief Inspector David Rowe," she said, "and this is Mr Hever." "Lever, Gregory Lever," the man corrected her. Pointing to the dog, he said, "And that's Daisy."

---

65 decline: Abhang  66 lay-by: Parkbucht  67 DS (Detective Sergeant): Rang bei der britischen Kriminalpolizei
68 to relate to s.th.: sich in etw. hineinversetzen können

"Did you see what happened?" David asked. "Not exactly," Gregory Lever replied. "I saw the lights of two cars from up there," he pointed up the hillside, "then I heard a crash and went to have a look."

David posed a number of questions and the elderly man explained more fully. He had difficulty sleeping and, at about three in the morning, had been taking Daisy for a short walk ("she's getting on[69] a bit and is, uh, incontinent, so I thought I'd take her out for a leak[70]," he explained). His house was at the edge of the village and he was walking along the path at the top of the hill, when he saw the lights of two cars in the lay-by next to the road down below. He could not remember seeing anyone in or next to the cars, but the lay-by had been some way off, so he only stopped for a moment and then followed his dog. Continuing on his way, he heard a strange noise, something big hurtling[71] downwards and then hitting something. He turned to look. The only thing he saw was a car driving away, but, being sure that there had been two cars and he hadn't heard another one leaving, he scrambled down the hill and, it almost being a full moon, could make out a crashed car down in the valley. "That's when I called 999[72]," Gregory concluded.

"It's a piece of luck that you were here," David said and thanked Gregory Lever. "It's our job now to find out what happened." The man was obviously reluctant to leave, but after some persuading from DS Johnstone he went home.

### Exercise 19

**Expressions connected with crime**

There are lots of informal or slang expressions concerning crimes and solving them. In the following groups of three, find the very informal (or slang) verbs or idioms.

1. a) to do s.o. in – b) to murder s.o. – c) to snuff s.o.
2. a) to kick the bucket – b) to bite the dust – c) to pass away – d) to die
3. a) to betray s.o. – b) to grass s.o. up – c) to shop s.o.
4. a) to take s.o. in – b) to arrest s.o. – c) to nick s.o.
5. a) to come clean – b) to fess up – c) to confess

---

69 to get on: älter werden  70 to take a dog out for a leak: mit einem Hund Gassi gehen  71 to hurtle down: herunterrasen, -stürzen  72 999: die britische Notrufnummer

Minutes later, crime scene manager Keith Lambert scrambled up to the lay-by. He gave a perfunctory[73] smile and David was somehow glad to see that Keith was also looking very tired. "Anything you can tell us?" he asked.

"It's too early to say," Keith replied, "but we're definitely going to have a closer look. And I'd recommend a full autopsy on the body. You see, the driver could have wanted to go back to the road and went into reverse[74] by mistake. But he'd have switched on the lights and the strange thing is that they're out. It could of course have happened during the fall, but …" "But lights don't switch themselves off that easily?" David asked. Keith nodded. "So someone else could have switched them off to make sure that the car was not found at once – to get away from the scene of a crime maybe?" Keith Lambert nodded again. "Is there any identification on the body?" "We've found a wallet," Keith said, "with the driver's licence, a credit card and an Equity card[75], so the deceased[76] must have been an actor. The name is Alan Gibson."

## Exercise 20

### Translate and find the idioms and phrasal verbs

Have another look at Exercise 19. Find one German translation for all of the verbs/phrases in each group. In all the groups, underline the idioms and the phrasal verbs (verb + preposition). Idioms and phrasal verbs are particularly often used in spoken and informal language.

---

73 perfunctory: flüchtig, der Form halber  74 to go into reverse: den Rückwärtsgang einlegen  75 Equity card: Ausweiskarte der Schauspielergewerkschaft (Equity)  76 the deceased: der Verstorbene

# Chapter 3

David phoned Emilia at about seven in the morning. The investigation of Alan Gibson's death had begun – his body had been carried to the mortuary[1] and was awaiting autopsy, and the SOCOs[2] (chagrined[3] about not realising in time that the lay-by they had been parking their cars in might have been the scene of a crime) had continued their work – but the police had not yet been able to find any next of kin[4]. A quick Internet search had confirmed that Gibson was indeed a member of the cast filming in St Stephen, so they had tried to contact Balmaha Entertainment, but it was still too early. David hoped that Emilia could help him. She had spent the last few weeks practically on site[5] and might know whom to phone.

"Why are you calling so early?" Emilia sounded cross[6], as if she had not yet got out of bed. David briefly explained that they had found a crashed car with the body of an actor and had not been able to notify anyone of his death. "His name was Alan Gibson," he said tentatively. "Alan? Oh no," he heard Emilia say faintly[7].

"Emilia?" David asked when the silence at the other end of the line seemed to become very long. "I'm alright," Emilia said, "it is only that I knew him. In fact I saw him just last night." There was another pause. "Where did the accident take place?" she asked then, sounding a bit more like her normal self. "He was found in a crashed car near Moreton," David replied and made a quick decision. "Emilia, would you mind if I stopped by?" he asked. This would give her a few minutes to compose herself[8] and he knew that a phone conversation was not the best way to pose the questions he wanted to ask. "Give me half an hour," was all she said.

When David arrived at Emilia and Robert's house, Emilia seemed to have got over her initial shock. She asked him into the kitchen, where Robert wordlessly handed him a cup of coffee. Gratefully, David took a few sips.

"Did you know Alan Gibson well?" he then asked Emilia. "Not that well," she replied. "He waited for his scenes in Robert's office, like some of

---

1 mortuary: Leichenschauhaus  2 SOCOs (Scene of Crime Officers): Spurensicherung  3 chagrined: verärgert
4 next of kin: nächste Angehörige  5 on site: (hier) am Ort des Geschehens  6 cross: missmutig, ärgerlich
7 faint: leise, kraftlos  8 to compose oneself: sich beruhigen

the others. It's been a nice diversion for me." "And somehow it's interesting to get to know people you've seen on TV," she added almost defensively. "If you need to contact someone at Balmaha Entertainment, I can text[9] you the number of Kathleen Cochrane's mobile. She is the second AD and will know who to contact." "I'll phone her when I'm back at the station," David said. "You said that you saw the deceased last night? Where was that?"

### Exercise 21

#### On the phone

Imagine another phone conversation, with David not telling Emilia of Alan Gibson's death, but asking to see her. Put the sentences in the correct order.

1. *Alright. See you in half an hour.*
2. *Bye.*
3. *Emilia? This is David.*
4. *Of course you may, but give me half an hour.*
5. *Hello?*
6. *I'm afraid that something has come up. I'd like to stop by if I may.*
7. *Oh, hello David. Why are you phoning so early?*
8. *Yes, see you then. Bye.*

Emilia explained that Nicholas Trent had invited cast and crew and some others to a party in the house that he, Ivor and Jessica had rented. "I took Charles," she said, "and it was a nice party." "Did you notice any quarrels?" Emilia frowned. "No, I didn't," she said "Not even a slight disagreement about something which could be important?" Emilia shook her head. "You might also want to ask Charles," she said. "We spoke to different people. But David, why are you asking these questions?"

David sighed. "It's too early to tell," he said, "but by sheer coincidence[10] we have a witness[11] who heard the crash and then heard another

9 to text s.o.: jmd. eine SMS schreiben  10 sheer coincidence: reiner Zufall  11 witness: Zeuge

car driving away. And who, shortly before, had seen two cars in the lay-by above the site of the crash." She looked at him aghast[12]. "You mean that … someone left Alan to his fate[13]? Or … even worse?" David nodded. "I see," Emilia said. Then she suddenly looked as if she had a toothache.

Exercise 22

### Symptoms of illness

Emilia only looks as if she has a toothache. Let's hope that you never suffer from the following symptoms.

Combine the sentences and phrases 1 to 6 and a to f, so that each combination forms a meaningful statement.

1. Can you recommend some nose drops?
2. I have got a splitting
3. I've been vomiting the whole night.
4. I've got chest pains.
5. My nose
6. One of my molars hurts.

a) headache.
b) I fear I have suffered a heart attack.
c) is running.
d) It's terrible to have a toothache.
e) My nose is blocked.
f) What can I do to get rid of this nasty gastric flu?

"David," she said. "You have to phone Kathy right now. I think that the police and some people from Balmaha have to meet at once." "Why?"

12 aghast: entsetzt  13 to leave s.o. to his fate: jmd. seinem Schicksal überlassen

David did not understand at first, but what Emilia said next made him catch his breath[14].

"Because today there's a really big get-together with journalists. There haven't been any media events so far, so every journalist will be virtually[15] panting[16] for information about the new TV series – and I don't even want to imagine what they could make of Alan's death. You have to decide what can be said about it."

David groaned – the media attention after the most recent murder in St Stephen had caused the police no end of trouble. "When does it begin?" he asked feebly[17]. "At 11 a.m.," Emilia replied, "there's an introductory event in the big function room[18] of the Swan Hotel, where the actors are staying, or most of them anyway. Afterwards the journalists will have the opportunity to talk to individual actors and to have a look at some of the locations."

A mere glimpse at his watch made David get up from his chair. "Have you sent me that text with the phone number? And is Kathleen Whatshername staying at the Swan as well?" Emilia nodded. "We've got less than three hours to come up with some kind of plan. We cannot have the media interfere[19] in the police investigation." He quickly said goodbye, adding that he would try to stop by in the evening, if at all possible.

### Exercise 23

**Frequently used phrases**

In this chapter so far, find the phrases for

1. (morgens) aufstehen – 2. Ich verstehe. – 3. jmd. eine SMS schicken – 4. reiner Zufall – 5. sich einen Plan ausdenken – 6. sich verabschieden – 7. Würde es dir etwas ausmachen?

Not an hour later, David, his superior DCS[20] Rupert Stevenson, director James Riddell, first and second AD Kathleen Cochrane and Christopher Cox and Balmaha Entertainment's press officer[21] Jacob Francis met in a small conference room in the Swan Hotel. A conference call[22] was being set up, so that producer Ann Staggard – who, on behalf[23] of Balmaha Entertainment, had co-developed the whole series and acquired the funds to finance it – could

---

14 to catch one's breath: den Atem anhalten  15 virtually: praktisch  16 to pant for s.th.: nach etw. lechzen  17 feeble: schwach, mit schwacher Stimme  18 function room: Veranstaltungsraum  19 to interfere in s.th.: sich in etw. einmischen  20 DCS (Detective Chief Superintendent): höherer Rang bei der britischen Kriminalpolizei  21 press officer: Pressereferent  22 conference call: Telefonkonferenz

also take part in what, David was sure, would have to be a meticulous piece of crisis management. Everyone was shocked, James Riddell's haggard[24] face was ashen[25], Kathleen Cochrane had obviously been crying, and Christopher Cox looked as if he could hardly believe what he had just been told.

Soon, a woman's voice could be heard via a loudspeaker. Ann Staggard said that she was devastated[26] about what had happened. Then there was a flurry[27] of questions. "What has to be done now?" "What happens to the production?" "Can we simply go on?" "What about Alan's part? – less than half of his scenes are in the can[28]." Rupert Stevenson looked at David. Give them a minute, the expression on his face said.

"We've got little more than two hours," Jacob Francis finally stated, "and there are lots of things we cannot decide right now. But we have to decide on a strategy in dealing with the press. Could we perhaps hear the police first and then maybe come up with suggestions ourselves?"

Exercise 24

### Phrasal verbs

Phrasal verbs (verb + preposition like "get in", "get by") are often used in more informal language, especially in spoken language. Underline the phrasal verbs in the next two paragraphs.

Rupert Stevenson did not have to be told twice. "I understand that soon there will be about fifty journalists in this hotel," he began. "We've had trouble with the press only recently, and I'm afraid that feeding the journalists a meagre[29] press release about the death of a member of the cast might not be enough. They could try to find out things for themselves, which might hinder[30] the police investigation. They might also pester[31] the cast and crew about Alan Gibson."

"So what would your suggestion be?" Christopher Cox asked. "I'd suggest starting off the media event with a statement about Mr Gibson having died this night in a tragic car accident. You should provide enough information about the deceased to satisfy the journalists, about his life, his career as an actor and so on. But don't let out anything about the police investigation that is going on and that we are not wholly satisfied. Make it

---

23 on behalf of: im Auftrag/Namen von  24 haggard: hager  25 ashen: aschgrau, kreidebleich  26 devastated: am Boden zerstört  27 flurry: Menge, Welle  28 in the can (Filmsprache): im Kasten  29 meagre: mager, armselig  30 to hinder: behindern, aufhalten  31 to pester: belästigen

sound like a straightforward[32] accident. You don't know the exact location of where it happened, you don't know whether there was alcohol involved. Then try to keep the press occupied – that means do not call off the tour of the locations. It would be good if Mr Riddell and some of the actors were able to go through[33] with the interviews as well. And it might be best if the actors were not told about the probable nature of Mr Gibson's death yet, and if we put off starting the police interviews until this evening. That way we can hope to keep the media under control."

### Exercise 25

Make phrasal verbs

To complete the next three paragraphs, make five phrasal verbs from the following verbs and prepositions.

Verbs: *draw – get – go – step – turn*

Prepositions: *in – out – over – through – up*

Nobody said a word. "That sounds sensible," Ann Staggard then said. "There is no way we can stop filming, there is too much money involved, too many jobs. We have to see if we can suspend[34] production, but if I remember correctly there was to be a break anyway." James Riddell confirmed this. "Filming was due to begin again next Monday," he said. "That's good," Ann replied, "so everyone has time to _____ (1) the shock, and the police can make their inquiries. I sincerely hope that it _____ (2) to have been an accident after all." "So do I," Christopher Cox said.

"So the first thing to do is to _____ (3) a press release stating that Alan Gibson died in a tragic car accident," Kathleen Cochrane said. "This is important, but I'd be grateful if you informed the actors first," David answered. "They have to have some time to deal with Mr Gibson's death and to decide if they want to _____ (4) with an interview." Kathleen nodded. "So the press release comes second." "Yes, and I'd like to have a quick look at the text you've decided on." "Of course," Kathleen said, but David thought that she was not very pleased.

32 straightforward: eindeutig  33 to go through with s.th.: etw. durchziehen  34 to suspend: (hier) aufschieben

"Another thing DCS Stevenson and I have decided on," David continued, "is that I, as SIO[35], need to be at the press conference. It would not be advisable for me to be in the room – I want to avoid being recognised as a member of the police, but I'd like to be able to gauge[36] the reaction of the media myself. And I'd like to establish a line of communication with Mr Francis, to be able to _____ (5) if there are difficult questions – I should say *when* there are difficult questions …" This time it was Jacob Francis who did not look pleased, but he nodded. "If you think that is going to help," he said, "why not?"

### Exercise 26

### In a meeting

Review the paragraphs describing the meeting between the police and members of the film crew. Underline the sentence(s) that

1. *point(s) out the aim of the meeting*
2. *make(s) suggestions as to how to structure it*
3. *ask(s) for a suggestion on how to deal with the problem*
4. *agree(s) with something*
5. *only lukewarmly[37] agree(s) with something*
6. *disagree(s) with something (very politely)*

The big room in the Swan Hotel was packed and the tension[38] was tangible[39], even in the small room where David and Kathy Cochrane were sitting. Word that someone had died had got out and David was only too glad that he did not have to take the press conference himself. As SIO he sometimes had to and he liked to think that he had developed a certain routine – but this was something else entirely!

"Two minutes," Kathy said. She had acted in a very professional manner, David thought, but having to tell many of the actors about Alan Gibson's death had taken its toll[40]. Now she was exhausted and looked very sad.

---

35 SIO (Senior Investigating Officer): Ermittlungsleiter  36 to gauge: einschätzen  37 lukewarm: (hier) halbherzig  38 tension: Spannung  39 tangible: spürbar  40 to take its toll: Spuren hinterlassen

An audio connection had been established between David and Jacob Francis, who was wearing an earpiece[41], and in the room where David was sitting a monitor had been installed. On it, David saw Jacob Francis and James Riddell entering the big conference room, where suddenly there was complete silence. James took a seat at the front, while Jacob stationed himself behind a microphone.

"I'd have liked to welcome you to an exciting day full of information about our new TV series," he said, "but last night a most tragic accident occurred …" In a few simple sentences, he told the audience that Alan Gibson had died in a car accident.

"You will understand that we are all devastated and that the day cannot proceed as planned," he then explained. "You will still be able to tour the locations and in the afternoon you will even be able to speak to a few of the actors. There won't be any one-to-one talks, however, but another press conference with those of the actors who feel up[42] to it. I do hope that you understand. But first James is going to say a few words about Alan, who will be very much missed by us all."

### Exercise 27

Reported speech (present tense)

In many conversations you have to reproduce what someone else has said. This needs to be done by using reported (or indirect) speech.

Put yourself in the shoes of a TV reporter making a live broadcast[43] about the press conference, who wants to reproduce what Jacob Francis says in the last paragraph. Rephrase this paragraph in reported speech. Begin with: "Jacob Francis says that we will understand that they are all devastated …" Do not always use "says", but look for different verbs.

Note: When using indirect speech in the present tense, the tense of the verbs does not change, but you might have to change other words (depending on who is speaking: "we" in direct speech, for example, becomes "they" in indirect speech etc.).

---

[41] earpiece: (versteckter) Ohrhörer  [42] to feel up to s.th.: sich zu etw. in der Lage fühlen  [43] live broadcast: Live-Übertragung

James Riddell took the microphone. "I knew Alan Gibson for almost ten years," he began. "I directed several films he acted in and I would have liked to see him in a leading role …" He continued by outlining the career of the deceased, throwing in his memories of Alan, things he had done and said and painting a very sympathetic picture of the dead man.

It was a clever speech, David thought. The director had hardly had any time to prepare, but what he was saying sounded as comprehensive[44] and as thoughtful as any obituary[45] prepared well in advance by one of the broadsheets[46]. David realised that James Riddell was a man who knew exactly what his audience expected and was able to deliver[47] it and who left absolutely nothing to chance – essential skills for being a successful director, he told himself. But what would a man like this do if someone crossed him? "He's got them all spellbound[48]," Kathy Cochrane, next to him, said quietly. David nodded.

James Riddell spoke for almost thirty minutes, not mentioning anything that could have a bearing[49] on the police investigation. He concluded by expressing his shock and disbelief about Alan Gibson's sudden death. "Filming will resume in a few days," he said, conveniently leaving out the fact that the break had been planned long before. "We cannot go on at once, but go on we must. And I think that Alan would have been among the first to say so." After a short silence, there was applause for what everybody seemed to agree was a heartfelt tribute[50] to the dead actor.

**Exercise 28**

### Reported speech (past tense)

You are a newspaper reporter and write an article telling your readers what James Riddell said yesterday. Take the quote[51] from the last paragraph and rewrite it in reported speech. Begin with: "James Riddell said that …"

Note: When using reported speech in the past tense, the tense of the verbs also has to be changed.

Then the journalists began to ask their questions. Fortunately, Jacob Francis and James Riddell were able to answer most of them at once. David only

44 comprehensive: vollständig  45 obituary: Nachruf  46 broadsheet: seriöse Zeitung  47 to deliver: (hier) Versprochenes halten  48 to have s.o. spellbound: jmd. in seinen Bann ziehen  49 to have a bearing on s.th.: für etw. Belang haben  50 tribute: Hommage  51 quote: Zitat

had to prompt[52] them twice to say that, Mr Gibson's death being a fatal accident, there would be an inquest[53] as a matter of course[54], and that, for the same reason, the police would investigate. And obviously the press was much more interested in the question of how the filming was going to proceed. Was there to be any reshooting[55]? Who would take Alan Gibson's role? James Riddell spoke at length[56] about the difficulties involved, often mentioning Alan's exceptional talent. When there were no further questions, James, again very cleverly, segued[57] into discussing the TV series itself. So the first hour of the press event ended comparatively uneventfully[58], with James announcing another talk about his ideas as a director at the end of the day. He bought us time, David thought. He only hoped that the journalists would be satisfied with what they had been given.

### Exercise 29

#### To chair a meeting

Note which of the following phrases or questions, which are often heard during meetings, lead from one point of the agenda to another (a) and which ones are a reply to what somebody has said (b). Some can be both (c).

1. *Ms Smith, could you sum up the current state of affairs?*
2. *I agree with your view of the situation.*
3. *I'm glad that you mentioned that. Now, could you explain in more detail …*
4. *It has been interesting to hear your opinion on the matter.*
5. *That was an excellent presentation. Thank you very much.*
6. *This was very interesting, but we also might want to think about another aspect of the problem.*
7. *Are there any suggestions as to how to solve this problem?*
8. *I'd very much like to hear what you all think.*

---

52 to prompt: soufflieren  53 inquest: gerichtliche Untersuchung (eines Todesfalls)  54 as a matter of course: selbstverständlich  55 to reshoot: neu filmen  56 at length: ausführlich  57 to segue into: überleiten zu  58 uneventful: ohne besondere Vorkommnisse

**Exercise 30**

**Translate**

1. *Rein zufällig rief er sie an, kurz bevor sie das Haus verließ.*

2. *David war froh, dass sich Kathy sehr professionell verhielt.*

3. *Wenn er auch kaum Zeit gehabt hatte, sich vorzubereiten, redete er ungefähr 30 Minuten lang.*

# Chapter 4

David could neither be present during the buffet lunch served to the journalists, nor could he take part in the tour of the film locations afterwards. It would not have been advisable, although he would have liked to hear what the journalists, among themselves, made of Alan Gibson's death. So he and DS Maud Johnstone, aided by Kathleen Cochrane, set up a room in the Swan Hotel and a schedule for a possible interviewing of the actors in the evening, when, everyone thought, the journalists would have left St Stephen. "I hope that there won't be any reason for these interviews after all," Kathleen confessed, "the situation is terrible as it is." David silently agreed. The last thing he wanted was to have another murder case on his hands. The St Stephen police had been understaffed for some time, but he had really hoped for a few weeks with something at least resembling normal working hours and with some kind of private life.

In the late afternoon, however, the forensic pathologist's[1] preliminary report[2] put an end to these hopes. In the police station David received a short phone call. "The face and the body of the deceased were badly damaged in the car crash," Dr Crewe explained, "but that damage was inflicted[3] post-mortem[4]. There are also some minor injuries he could have incurred in a fight shortly before his death. Most importantly, there is considerable damage at the lower back of the skull[5], which we think was the cause of death, but which is not consistent with the injuries caused by the car crash. We cannot be one hundred percent sure yet and there are still lots of tests to be done, but I'd treat this death as suspicious."

"When did Mr Gibson die or is it too early to say?" David asked. "Between two and four in the morning, I estimate[6]," Dr Crewe replied. David nodded. The 999 call had come in at about half past three, so that tallied[7]. He asked for the preliminary report to be e-mailed to him, ended the call and, together with Maud Johnstone, returned to the Swan Hotel. He wanted to witness the last parts of the events scheduled for the media and intended to begin questioning actors and crew members shortly afterwards.

---

1 forensic pathologist: Gerichtsmediziner  2 preliminary report: vorläufiger Bericht  3 to inflict: zufügen  4 post-mortem: nach Eintreten des Todes  5 skull: Schädel  6 to estimate: (ein)schätzen  7 to tally: zusammenpassen

## Exercise 31

### Answer the questions

Answer the following questions. Do not write your answers down, but try to speak them aloud. If this is difficult, read the answers suggested in the key to the exercises and reproduce them as if you were talking to somebody.

1. *What does David do between the two media events at the Swan Hotel?*
2. *How does the forensic pathologist confirm everyone's fears about Alan Gibson's death?*
3. *Why does David return to the Swan Hotel?*

The journalists had probably looked forward to meeting the actors, but in its changed form the get-together was a subdued[8] affair. Present were Ivor Byrnes, Leo Sandys, Jean Whyte, Jessica Sleightholme and Nora Palliser. David remembered a film with Ivor Byrnes, but it was the first time he saw the other actors. They all seemed composed – but while Ivor Byrnes's face was inscrutable[9], Nora Palliser looked as if what had happened affected[10] her deeply. David had heard that she had decided that, as the heroine, she shouldn't bow out[11]. Now he realised that her hair was the same colour as Alix's and was suddenly filled with longing[12]. He had planned to go to London for the weekend, but now that wouldn't be possible.

It soon became clear that the journalists had by no means[13] had their fill[14] of asking questions about Alan Gibson. Jacob Francis had to fend off[15] a number of inquisitive[16] questions not pertaining[17] to the new TV series, which he did skilfully. But some members of the press were persistent[18] and would suddenly bring up Alan Gibson.

A female reporter, whose face David did not see on the monitor, was particularly obnoxious[19] towards Nora Palliser. "As a modern Elizabeth Bennet, you would be more independent and maybe more adventurous[20]," she said, "so before Darcy comes along, you could have something going on with other men." "I cannot give away too much of the plot, so I'm afraid that you'll have to wait until the series is out," Nora replied diplomatically, "but of course a modern Elizabeth Bennet has more opportunities than …"

8 subdued: gedämpft  9 inscrutable: undurchschaubar  10 to affect: (emotional) betreffen  11 to bow out: etwas (da es nun einen guten Grund gibt) nicht tun  12 longing: Sehnsucht  13 by no means: auf keinen Fall  14 to have one's fill of s.th.: genug von etw. haben  15 to fend off: abwehren  16 inquisitive: neugierig  17 to pertain: (logisch) betreffen  18 persistent: hartnäckig  19 obnoxious: widerwärtig  20 adventurous: abenteuerlustig

"I'm sure that she has her pick[21] of men," the journalist interrupted, "and am I wrong in assuming that there was a certain chemistry between you and Alan Gibson, Miss[22] Palliser? How do you feel about his death?" David noticed that Nora had to swallow hard and that her eyes filled with tears. Ivor Byrnes put his hand on her arm and glared[23] at the reporter, then there were some flashlights and all Jacob Francis could do was to call up another journalist who posed a less offensive question.

The event did not take as long as planned – everyone could see that the journalists were not really interested in what the actors had to say and that the actors' hearts were not in it. So James Riddell took things into his own hands and began the talk he had announced in the morning. Some of the journalists left soon afterwards, but others stayed and in the end there was even a short discussion that really focussed[24] on *The Lives and Loves of the Bennet Sisters*.

### Exercise 32

#### Literary and media terms

Complete an excerpt from James's speech, using the terms

*cliffhanger – culmination points – filmmakers – light entertainment – literary form – novel – soap opera – story threads – suspense – TV format – viewer*

*In Jane Austen's day, many thought the _____ (1) a _____ (2) of dubious merit, and nowadays many do not consider the _____ (3) a _____ (4) to be taken seriously. I beg to differ. While it is true that many soap operas offer not much more than _____ (5), they have many characteristics that make them appealing to the _____ (6) – characteristics that _____ (7) in general do well to emulate. There are, for example, always various _____ (8), which do not all end at the same time. So for the story as a whole, various _____ (9) are possible. In the* **Bennet Sisters** *we do something quite similar in covering the lives of all the Bennet sisters, which, of course, do not develop synchronously. Another soap opera device to create _____ (10) is the _____ (11). You'll have to wait and see how we use it!*

---

21 to have one's pick of s.th.: sich etw. aussuchen können  22 Miss: noch immer verwendete (inzwischen aber etwas überholte) Anrede von Schauspielerinnen  23 to glare: wütend anstarren  24 to focus on s.th.: sich auf etw. konzentrieren

When the police began their interviews, cast and crew had been made aware that Alan Gibson's death had not been an accident. All hoped for a short respite[25] before the general public and the media had to learn of this, but David knew that it wouldn't be long. At least the SOCOs had concluded their investigation of the crime scene and most of the journalists had left town again.

"We can only hope that most of them will not return," James Riddell said. The director had asked to be the first to be interviewed. He would have to leave the same evening to promote another film, but had promised to be available whenever the police needed him.

James had nothing to say about the night of the murder – he and his film editor[26] had reviewed the shooting of the day to ensure that no scenes had to be repeated, like they had done every evening. So he had not been able to attend the party. Concerning the deceased, he had not noticed any arguments or anything out of the ordinary in the weeks before.

"It may sound strange, but I have to get to know Mr Gibson," David said, "and from your speech this morning you knew him very well. What I did not quite understand was the nature of your relationship. Was it mainly professional, or did you consider him a personal friend?" "We were friendly, yes," James answered, "but not close friends. It was a professional friendship."

David was not wholly convinced. There had been something in what James had said in the morning he could not quite put his finger on[27], but it might be worth a try. "You first described the man you knew very warmly," he said. "Concerning the project you're working on now, your praise was more objective, it was mainly for the actor, for the professional. Was there a special reason for that?"

James Riddell gave him a long look. "So you noticed," he said. "I have no objection[28] against telling you more about Alan. In fact, I can see that you might consider it important." He paused. "When Alan and I first met, he was an unknown, but very promising young actor and I was trying to find funding[29] for my first film. We helped each other. He worked for very little money and I cast him in some of my films. We were real friends then, personal friends."

"Then Alan began to drink. First it was to relax, then it was to forget his money problems, then he became an addict[30]. Sometimes he couldn't

---

25 respite: Atempause  26 film editor: für den Filmschnitt Verantwortlicher  27 to put one's finger on s.th.: etw. genau ausmachen  28 objection: Einwand  29 funding: Geldmittel  30 addict: Süchtiger

work, and nobody wants an actor who is unreliable[31]. He sought professional help, although it took him a long time to recover. I tried to help, but it is difficult to stay friends with an alcoholic. We kept in touch, but ... I suppose you could say that I distanced myself from him." "Last year, he came to see me and said that he was better, but that he needed something to keep him going, to help him to finally overcome[32] his addiction. He had spent some time in rehab[33]. I spoke to the doctor he was seeing and decided to give him a chance. Alan was a great actor and he was exactly the person I imagined for the role of Andrew Fitzwilliam. He did not disappoint me and I was glad. But now ..." James was silent.

"There isn't any chance that he was drunk and caused some freak accident[34]?" he asked. "I'm afraid not," David said.

### Exercise 33

Scrambled sentences

Put the words into the correct order.

1. keep going needed he him help some to
2. know Mr Gibson I get have to to
3. recover time took it quite him to some

That Alan Gibson had gone through a bad time was corroborated[35] by Kathleen Cochrane. "He told me about his alcohol problem," she said, "and that he had worked very hard to gain control of it. But in this respect he seemed fine to me." "In this respect?" David probed. "It cannot have been easy in an environment[36] like ours," Kathleen explained, "and when I think of last night's party, it must have been really hard. I'm sure that Nicholas didn't know, and I wouldn't have liked to tell him about Alan's problem, but why didn't I think of giving him a hint? All that booze[37] ... it could have been displayed[38] a bit less openly." She seemed upset. "I didn't see Alan drinking, but maybe he did after all?" she asked.

Again David had to say that what had happened had not been alcohol-related – but maybe Alan's not being able to drink had triggered[39]

---

31 unreliable: unzuverlässig  32 to overcome s.th.: über etw. hinwegkommen  33 to spend time in rehab: eine Entziehungskur machen  34 freak accident: durch einen seltsamen Zufall bedingter Unfall  35 to corroborate: bestätigen  36 environment: (hier) Umfeld  37 booze (ugs.): Alkohol  38 to display: zur Schau stellen  39 to trigger: auslösen

something? He asked Kathleen if Alan had behaved differently than usual, but she couldn't think of anything. "And when did you leave the party?" "I don't exactly know," she said. "I remember looking at my watch and seeing that it was after midnight. I knew that I wouldn't be able to sleep in today, so I decided to leave soon. Which I did, but I do not remember the exact time." "Did you leave alone or with someone else?" "No, I drove myself back to the hotel alone." David decided to leave it at that for now.

### Exercise 34

**Find the questions …**

… and ask them by speaking them aloud.

1. _____? – *No, I didn't see him touch any alcohol.*
2. _____? – *I left after midnight, but not long after that.*
3. _____? – *No, nobody was. I was alone when I drove back to the hotel.*

Christopher Cox thoughtfully answered all of David's questions and, it seemed to David, tried to be helpful. But he eventually[40] admitted that he hadn't known the dead man very well. "Kathy might have known him better," he said, "but then she's more involved in the organisational side of the business, in keeping the actors happy." And he couldn't say anything about what might have happened later on at the party. "I was knackered," he declared, "so I left at about half past eleven and went back to the hotel. It was certainly before midnight."

Next on David's agenda[41] was to begin questioning the actors, who had only been told that Alan Gibson's death was probably not the result of an accident after the press conference. Ivor Byrnes had volunteered to be first. David suspected that neither he nor Maud Johnstone were entirely uncurious about the famous actor and was a bit wary[42] of being influenced by that.

40 eventually: schließlich  41 agenda: (hier) Programm  42 wary: skeptisch

He need not have worried. Ivor's behaviour was absolutely professional, and absolutely neutral, as he answered all of the questions put to him about the night of the murder and his relationship with the deceased. He had worked with Alan before, in another film, about two years ago. He had known the murdered man, but not very well. Their interactions had not been of a personal kind. Did he like him? Ivor Byrnes gave a wry[43] smile to Maud's question. "He was easy to get along with," he said, "but to like? I don't like people easily, I'm afraid."

At last there was a small chink in Ivor Byrnes's armour[44] of impersonality, David thought, but his reply did not exactly answer the question. He pointed this out and Ivor reconsidered. "I neither liked him nor had anything against him. We got along fine and I do not think that either of us expected anything else from the other. But I am sorry that he is dead. He was a talented actor."

### Exercise 35

Translate

1. Er hätte sich keine Sorgen machen müssen, dass die Pressekonferenz nicht stattfinden würde.

2. Die Filmproduktionsgesellschaft musste die Journalisten bei Laune halten.

3. Jacob Francis musste eine Anzahl neugieriger Fragen abwehren.

While Ivor Byrnes and Christopher Cox had not shown much emotion, Leo Sandys was the exact opposite. From his behaviour at the press conference, David would not have thought him distraught[45] about Alan Gibson's death, but the news that Alan was probably the victim of a murder seemed to be too much for him to stomach[46]. Leo was silently crying during the whole of the short interview, and they hardly got a rational answer out of him. Maud finally walked him to his room. "Poor boy," she said when she came back. "Let's hope that he will be better tomorrow."

---

43 wry: (hier) säuerlich, ironisch  44 chink in the armour: Riss in der Rüstung  45 distraught: außer sich  46 to stomach (fig.): vertragen, verdauen

Exercise 36

"Let", "have", "make" or "allow"?

Complete the sentences, choosing the English phrase that best fits the phrase in brackets, which includes the German word "lassen".

1. _____ to Nicholas's party. *(lasst uns gehen)*

2. She _____ for two hours. *(ihn warten lassen)*

3. The windscreen wipers of his car did not work, so he _____. *(sie reparieren lassen)*

4. I know you're busy, so _____. *(lass dich nicht von mir aufhalten[47])*

5. After staying in bed for four days, he was much better, so the doctor _____. *(ließ ihn aufstehen)*

Last on David's list was Nora Palliser, who Maud had originally thought they should talk to the following morning. Nora, however, had asked to be interviewed as early as possible. "She said that she wanted to be able to sleep tonight," Maud Johnstone told David, "and that it would help if she didn't have to think about a police interview in the morning. She would be very grateful." David, remembering that the actress had seemed exhausted by the end of the press conference, could sympathise with that. At the same time he feared another emotional outburst of the Leo Sandys kind.

But Nora Palliser impressed him favourably. She was still very much shocked, but calm enough to answer David and Maud's questions, making an effort to listen attentively and to give answers that were to the point. She told them about her relationship with Alan Gibson – which had been a purely professional one, she assured them. And she had been present until the end of the party. "I spent the night at the house," she said. "I had come in Ivor's car, straight from the filming, and had thought about catching a lift[48] back to the hotel. But in the end I stayed the night."

David made a mental note to have[49] Maud ask who had caught lifts with whom, who had stayed over, who might have had access to another

47 aufhalten: detain  48 to catch a lift: sich im Auto mitnehmen lassen  49 to have s.o. do s.th.: jmd. etw. tun lassen

person's car keys, and to find out if some people could give each other alibis for the night or the time of the murder. He did not really want to ask Nora this and, anyway, it might be better if these questions came from a woman … From the impression he had formed of the party, he could well imagine that some people had spent the night together – which, considering the number of people they had to interview, would certainly be helpful.

"So you stayed the night," he offered. "Did you speak to Alan Gibson or did you notice someone talking to him?" "I spoke to him several times," Nora replied. "But we were mostly bantering[50]. After weeks of filming, nobody was in the mood for serious discussions. Although …," she suddenly fell silent. "Although?" Maud asked.

"Alan and Kathy were discussing something," she said with obvious reluctance. "And that struck[51] you as odd?" David wanted to know. Nora said nothing, and he could see that she really did not want to answer his question.

"Kathy was upset," Nora finally said. "I got the impression that she was setting him right[52] about something. But then Kathy often is, it is her job," she hastened to add, "I'm sure that it was about nothing!" "Did you overhear anything that was said?" Maud asked. "Only snippets," Nora replied, hesitating again, "she said 'no way' and that something would be unprofessional. That is really all I overheard, you have to believe me!" Now she was visibly upset. David and Maud exchanged a glance. "Thank you for telling us," David said gently. He hoped that Nora Palliser would be able to sleep that night.

### Exercise 37

#### Saying thank you

There are many ways to say thank you. Which word or phrase would you use in 1. an informal situation, 2. when you are really grateful, 3. to say "no, thank you", 4. in a more formal situation, 5. if you want to be sarcastic?

*a)* Cheers! – *b)* I do appreciate this. – *c)* I'm fine. – *d)* I'm much obliged. – *e)* Ta. – *f)* I'm truly grateful. – *g)* Thanks a lot. – *h)* Thanks. – *i)* Thank you very much. – *j)* I'm good.

---

50 to banter: sich necken, scherzen  51 to strike: (hier) auffallen  52 to set s.o. right: jmd. die Meinung sagen

Emilia was glad when, shortly before ten, David phoned and asked if he could still stop by. After his quick visit in the morning she had been on tenterhooks[53] all day. She had called Charles and together with him had dissected[54] everything they had seen and heard the evening before. Charles had expressed an interest in being present if David dropped in, and so they were eagerly waiting to see what he could tell them.

First of all, however, David wanted to hear about what they had noticed at the party, and he wanted to hear it in great detail. After the briefest outline of how the journalists had been only told of Alan Gibson's death, both Charles and Emilia had to give a minute-to-minute account about what had happened in their presence the evening before. Both of them had spoken to many different people. Emilia gave an account of the *Pride and Prejudice*-discussion in the kitchen and Charles related[55] what he had told Dan Parker and Alison Reid about the trials and tribulations[56] of being a priest.

David listened, asked questions, but otherwise did not say much. Not that there would have been much to say – neither of them had witnessed any serious discussions or quarrels. The only thing David seemed to think of any interest was that Emilia had got the impression that Alan had been sticking to soft drinks, but she omitted to add that she had also formed the impression that he was looking for someone to spend the night with.

### Exercise 38

### Keeping a conversation going

While listening to Emilia and Charles, David has not been saying much, but he will have participated in the conversation by using phrases like the ones in the following list. Find the phrases that signal 1. agreement, 2. astonishment or that 3. steer the conversation in a certain direction.

*a) Could you explain …? – b) exactly – c) Do you recall …? – d) you're absolutely right – e) how very interesting – f) I know what you mean – g) indeed – h) My goodness! – i) Tell me more about … – j) that's incredible – k) that's true – l) that's weird*

---

53 on tenterhooks: auf glühenden Kohlen  54 to dissect: auseinandernehmen, sezieren  55 to relate: berichten  56 trials and tribulations: (etwa) Widrigkeiten

David then told them more about the combined efforts[57] of the police and film production team to make Alan Gibson's death appear to be an accident while St Stephen was teeming[58] with journalists, about the successful first press conference in the morning and the less successful one at the end of the journalists' event. "We'll have to go public about the murder tomorrow, with our own press conference," he sighed. "There are too many people around now who know about it. If someone connected to the filming or an employee of the Swan Hotel only gave as much as a hint to the media, there'd be hell to pay[59] …"

They then spoke about Alan Gibson, who David needed to gather as much information about as possible. "Now that I think of it, he hardly spoke about himself," Emilia said. "He was often talking nonsense, amusing nonsense. Anyway, most of the talk I've listened to in the last three weeks was a bit nonsensical, or about the filming or something else happening right then. Nobody had the time – or the energy – to talk about politics or relationships or the state of the arts or whatever. The only person I've been having real conversations with is Kathy Cochrane, even though we didn't spend that much time together – not half as much time as Alan spent in Robert's office." "Did Kathy tell you anything about Alan?" David asked. "Not much," Emilia replied, "she's usually very discreet. But wait … she said that Alan had had a rough time recently. She didn't say why, though."

She thought for a bit. "Don't make too much of it, David," she said, "but I got the impression that Alan and Ivor didn't care about each other much. Alan waited in Robert's office and Ivor made a point of waiting in the house next door. The production company has rented a large flat there to use as a make-up and costume studio, and one of the rooms was set up as a kind of common room[60] for the actors."

Charles had nothing to say concerning Alan Gibson. But he had formed a general impression about the actors and the members of the film production company. "Some were very nice, even charming," he said, "some less so, though everyone was polite. I think that most of them are too professional to show much of their feelings, not to outsiders like me, in any case." "Some may be a bit more difficult than others," Emilia said, "but there are no prima donnas among them, I'm glad to say." "I got the same impression today," David agreed, "but so far, I've only spoken to some of them."

57 combined efforts: vereinte Bemühungen  58 to teem with s.th.: von etw. wimmeln  59 there would be hell to pay (ugs.): es wäre der Teufel los  60 common room: Gemeinschaftsraum

### Exercise 39

## Idioms with "make"

Find the German equivalents for the English idioms.

*1. to make a face – 2. to make a killing – 3. to make a move – 4. to make a point – 5. to make free with s.th. – 6. to make light of s.th. – 7. to make short work of s.th. – 8. to make time for s.th. – 9. to make too much of s.th.*

*a) ein Argument anbringen – b) das Gesicht verziehen – c) etw. verharmlosen – d) etw. zu viel Bedeutung zumessen – e) mit etw. kurzen Prozess machen – f) sich auf den Weg machen – g) sich für etw. Zeit nehmen – h) etw. ausgiebig verwenden/konsumieren – i) viel Geld verdienen*

---

"Nora Palliser seems to be different," Charles said. "We talked a bit yesterday and I like her. She doesn't hide her real self. And you can tell that she is genuinely interested in people and cares about their feelings." He smiled mischievously at Emilia. "Do you think that there could be something between her and Ivor?" he asked her.

How typical of Charles! Despite the seriousness of the situation, Emilia had to suppress a smile. "Oh Charles," she said. "I honestly don't know. But even if there were – with all the media attention for Elizabeth and Darcy it would be _____ (1) to admit to something like that. I think that they are _____ (2) friends, and Nora seems to be one of the few who can draw Ivor out of his shell of superiority[61]. Did you talk to her, David? What did you make of her?"

"She was the last on today's list," David replied. "She seems to be very _____ (3)." This was a bit neutral for Emilia's taste, who had noticed that he had listened with interest to what she and Charles had just been saying. But she understood that David, as a police officer, could not tell others much about the state of the investigation. At the same time she dearly wished that he would!

She looked at David. Should she offer to help with this case? They had worked together before, but he had also warned her off[62] quite _____ (4) sometimes. I'd better not ask, she decided. But

---

61 superiority: Überlegenheit  62 to warn s.o. off: jmd. stark abraten

what harm could it do to talk to some of the people she had spent the last weeks with?

### Exercise 40

**Choose the adjectives**

Complete the two last paragraphs of this chapter by using adjectives from the following groups. Which adjectives do not fit?

1. *awkward – embarrassing – precarious*
2. *good – narrow – close*
3. *cute – nice – pleasant*
4. *sharply – cuttingly – severely*

# Chapter 5

Someone at the police station had once dubbed[1] DS Maud Johnstone the "queen of lists". The nickname[2], David thought, undervalued Maud's more important skills, but she herself admitted that she liked drawing up lists – she was a methodical person. When David entered the room at the Swan Hotel the next morning, Maud was poring over[3] some sheets of paper. "Good morning," she said and he knew that she wanted to share something.

"I've done a bit of comparing," Maud said, pointing to the papers on the desk. "We've begun a number of lists, including a list of the people who, after the party, returned to the hotel in their cars. We've also viewed the footage[4] of the CCTV camera[5] in the hotel's lobby[6]. It tells us when some of the guests returned from the party, the guests staying in the hotel's main house, that is. And I've discovered something interesting. Yesterday, Kathleen Cochrane claimed that she left the party not long after midnight – but it was 3.57 a.m. when she returned here. She took more than three hours to drive herself from near Moreton to St Stephen." "Which normally does not take any longer than thirty minutes," David said. Maud nodded. "She is said to have had a heated discussion with Alan Gibson," she pointed out. "And she arrived at the hotel about thirty minutes after the 999 call. Let's see her again," David decided.

Exercise 41

### Reading numbers aloud

How would you say these numbers or time designations[7] in a conversation?

1. *It was 3.32 a.m. when he called 999.*

2. *My phone number is 21 70 34. 44 77 22 was my old number.*

3. *Jane Austen wrote in the early 1800s.* Pride and Prejudice *was first published in 1813. From some dates and days of the week in the text (26 November, the night of the Netherfield ball, among them), it has been supposed that the action takes place in 1811 or 1812.*

---

1 to dub s.o.: jmd. einen Spitznamen geben  2 nickname: Spitzname  3 to pore over s.th.: in etw. vertieft sein
4 footage: Filmmaterial  5 CCTV (Closed Circuit TV) camera: Überwachungskamera  6 lobby: Rezeption
7 time designation: Zeitangabe

Kathy Cochrane was surprised to be called again – before lots of the others had even spoken to the police for a first time. And when David and Maud explained what someone else had overheard, she did not immediately give an answer. It was obvious that she had to do some thinking.

"It was Nora who told you, wasn't it?" she asked. "She was nearby when Alan and I were quarrelling, she must have heard everything." David did not want to explain what exactly had been overheard and by whom. "We need to hear what happened in your own words," he said.

"Alan made a pass[8] at me," Kathy finally said. "He wanted to get laid[9]. It was nothing personal, almost any woman would have done. He didn't fancy me, nor was he really my type, not in that way." She gave a sad smile.

"I was disappointed," she continued. "I had thought him a friend. There are, of course, lots of location flings[10], but if you have to boss people around like I do, it can become awkward to mix business and pleasure. So I told him that it would not be very professional for me to … you know, and I told him off quite forcefully, I'm afraid."

"Why didn't you tell us yesterday?" Maud wanted to know. "Because it wasn't important. And if Nora had heard the whole thing, as I thought she had, she wouldn't have thought it important either."

"What happened then?" David asked. "I left. I had thought about staying the night, but I was fed up and left." "And after you left? What did you do then?" he probed. Kathy stared at him. "I drove myself to the hotel," she stated matter-of-factly. "Ms Cochrane, it took you about three hours to get back here," David said softly.

Kathy went white, but this time she had an explanation to hand. "I did not want to tell you, oh God, I really hate to," she began. "I had only been on my way for a few minutes when I realised that I wasn't fit to drive. I had had quite a few glasses of wine, and I stupidly almost had a collision with a dry stone wall[11]. I parked the car on a track[12], got my sleeping bag – which I had brought in case I wanted to spend the night at the house – and slept on the backseat for an hour or two. I woke up because I felt terribly cramped. But I also felt more sober[13], so I returned to the hotel."

"You didn't notice anything on your route?" David inquired. Kathy gave a humourless smile. "I passed a lay-by where there were some cars, a van and a police car." "You didn't think of stopping?" Kathy shrugged her

---

8 to make a pass at s.o.: einen Annäherungsversuch bei jmd. machen  9 to get laid (ugs.): Sex haben  10 fling: kurze Affäre  11 dry stone wall: Trockenmauer aus Bruchsteinen  12 track: Feldweg  13 sober: nüchtern

shoulders. "You wouldn't have thanked me for it," she said. "I thought that there must have been some accident. And I only wanted to be back in the hotel and get some sleep. I was exhausted."

"Do you remember which track you parked your car in?" Maud showed Kathy an OS[14] map. "Here is the house," she said, "where did you park the car?" Kathy looked at the map for some time and followed the single-track road from the house with her finger. Then she shook her head. "I'm afraid I cannot tell." "Would you find it again if you went in your car?" David asked "I'm not sure. I doubt it," Kathy replied. "It was dark and I was not really in a state to notice things." "Can't you describe your surroundings? Was there a tree, a wall, a fence[15]?" "I only remember that there was an upward slope next to the driver's door, and a downward slope next to the other." "Weren't you afraid of sleeping on the moors – all on your own?" "I was afraid of causing serious damage to my car and to myself," Kathy was upset now.

David took her through everything she had said for a second time. She did not contradict herself, but how convenient that she did not remember anything specific! "Please stop by the police station this afternoon," he said at last. "We have to take a formal statement. And you must not leave St Stephen." "For God's sake!" Kathy protested. "I've told you several times and you made notes." David did not reply. He was sure that Kathleen Cochrane would be able to figure out why they needed to take another statement. "I expect you at the police station between half past three and four," Maud said. "I'll be there," Kathy said. "I hope you don't mind if I leave now. I've got things to do and I've got a splitting headache."

### Exercise 42

### Idioms and phrases with "take"

Find English equivalents for the German words or terms 1 to 8. All consist of the verb "to take" and another word (and, in some cases, also an article or a pronoun).

*1. abheben – 2. eine Aussage aufnehmen – 3. es mit der Angst zu tun bekommen – 4. es ruhig angehen lassen – 5. es als selbstverständlich ansehen – 6. sich Mühe geben – 7. sich ein Herz fassen – 8. Zeit benötigen/sich Zeit nehmen*

---

14 OS (Ordnance Survey): der geografische Dienst Großbritanniens  15 fence: Zaun

David and Maud continued with the interviews for the whole morning, questioning members of cast and crew and comparing information – but more than forty guests had been present at the party. Shortly before David had to leave for the press conference concerning Alan Gibson's murder, which would take place in the police station, Jacob Francis came in. Balmaha Entertainment's press officer was carrying a stack[16] of newspapers and other documents. "I thought you'd better see these," he said, spreading the papers on the table. "I'm afraid that there's a lot of interest in Alan's death."

David was taken aback. On the table there were approximately fifteen newspapers and many more sheets with what looked like press cuttings[17]. "These are the printouts of e-mails from our London office," Jacob explained. "Is there anything I really need to know?" David asked. "Well, there is this immense media interest," Jacob replied, "most of the papers have stuck to what we've told them, but some are printing every story they can get. Have a look at this." He handed David a copy[18] of the *Daily News*, a tabloid[19] David had always thought particularly lurid[20]. There were two photos of yesterday's press conference, a close-up[21] of Nora Palliser and a smaller one of her next to Ivor Byrnes. "Nora: tears for dead actor friend," the headline ran, and a second, smaller headline said, "But Ivor comforts her."

David scanned[22] the text and pulled a face[23]. "Thank you," he said. "It's good to know what to expect … What did Ms Palliser and Mr Byrnes say?" "It's probably not the worst they've had to deal with," Jacob replied. "Nora just shrugged her shoulders. She said that she didn't expect otherwise. I've had no opportunity to talk to Ivor yet, but he's here. Only a few minutes ago I saw him charging[24] across the corridor, with a face like thunder."

### Exercise 43

**Idioms with parts of the body**

Find the German equivalent to these English idioms:

*1. over s.o.'s head – 2. to be chucked out on one's ear – 3. to come to a head – 4. to do s.o.'s head in – 5. to drag one's feet – 6. to force s.o.'s hand – 7. to get out of hand – 8. to lend s.o. a hand – 9. to hear s.th. straight from the horse's mouth – 10. to pay through the nose – 11. to scream one's head off*

---

16 stack: Stapel  17 press cutting: Zeitungsausschnitt  18 copy: (hier) Exemplar  19 tabloid: Boulevardzeitung  20 lurid: reißerisch  21 close-up: Nahaufnahme  22 to scan: überfliegen  23 to pull a face: das Gesicht verziehen  24 to charge: (hier) stürmen

*a)* aus allererster Quelle erfahren – *b)* außer Kontrolle geraten – *c)* einen Wucherpreis bezahlen – *d)* hochkant herausfliegen – *e)* jmd. behilflich sein – *f)* jmd. gewaltig nerven – *g)* jmd. in Zugzwang bringen – *h)* sich die Lunge aus dem Hals schreien – *i)* sich zuspitzen – *j)* trödeln – *k)* über jmds. Kopf hinweg/zu hoch für jmd.

The hour following David's return to the police station was spent preparing for the press conference. David, police press officer Amal Bhat and DCS Rupert Stevenson worked on the exact wording of the statement that David, as SIO, would read, and quickly spoke about possible questions from the journalists.

Although David had had a bit of time to brace himself[25] for the onslaught[26] of the media and had been aware of the great interest in the death of Alan Gibson, he had not expected the sheer number of journalists who had managed to travel to St Stephen in the few hours since the East Yorkshire Police had announced the press conference. The station's conference room was crowded, there were TV cameras and not everyone had been able to find a seat. The desk in front of the blue screen with the badge[27] of the East Yorkshire Police was brightly lit and on it there were several microphones, pointing to where David and Amal Bath now sat down. David took a deep breath. This was not his favourite kind of situation!

When Amal Bath announced that the police were launching[28] a murder inquiry into the death of 36-year-old Alan Gibson, there was absolute silence. Amal quickly introduced David, who then read the statement that outlined what had happened, gave a brief account of the pathologist's findings and said what the police were doing.

"We are pursuing several lines of inquiry[29]," David added, "but we do not have a lead[30] yet. One thing we would very much like to know is what happened immediately before the car crash was fabricated[31]. We know that not many cars will have passed the lay-by near Moreton between one and half past three a.m. on November 27, but if somebody did and saw anything, we would be very glad if he or she came forward. Any piece of information, however unimportant it might appear, could be relevant."

25 to brace oneself: sich wappnen  26 onslaught: Ansturm  27 badge: Emblem  28 to launch: einleiten
29 line of inquiry: Ermittlungsrichtung  30 lead: Spur  31 to fabricate: fingieren

## Exercise 44

Asking people to do something

Rephrase the following sentences (which could be considered as rude[32] in a number of situations).

1. *If you saw something, tell us!*
2. *Find another day for our appointment!*
3. *My mobile's battery is flat, give me yours!*
4. *Explain this!*

by using modals and more polite expressions like

*Would you mind …, We'd be glad …, It would be very helpful …, I'd appreciate it if … I'm afraid that …*

---

When Amal Bhat announced a few minutes for questions, it was immediately clear that a short time would not suffice. David saw that the raised hands in the first rows of the audience alone were more than he could count.

There were questions about the fabricated accident and about the injuries Alan Gibson had incurred[33]. These were easy to reply to, but were followed by others requiring a more diplomatic answer.

"Are the cast and crew of the TV series that is being filmed your main line of inquiry?" a journalist working for a major news programme[34] wanted to know. "We are speaking to them, of course," David replied, "but also because we need to get to know Mr Gibson. As I pointed out before, we do not have any leads yet and our investigation is by no means restricted to this one group of people."

An elderly woman David recognised as the crime reporter of one of the broadsheets asked if there was any reason why Alan Gibson's murder had first been treated as a tragic accident. "My colleague from the arts pages[35] was here only yesterday, at Balmaha Entertainment's press day, and I cannot imagine that their way of presenting Mr Gibson's death had not been agreed on with the police," she said.

---

32 rude: unhöflich, grob  33 to incur: sich zuziehen  34 news programme: Nachrichtensendung  35 arts pages: Feuilleton

David cursed inwardly. He could have understood if a reproach[36] like this – for a reproach it was – had been made in the paper itself, but to hear it voiced right now was awkward and might give other journalists ideas. "We had to wait for conclusive findings on the pathologist's part," he replied. "And am I right in presuming that you didn't want all the media attention quite so soon?" the reporter said. "You will understand that in any investigation of a sudden death the first few hours are of the essence[37] and that the investigation itself has to be our first priority," David said. He thought of adding a sentence about the police trying to accommodate[38] the wishes of the media, but the less said about that the better, he decided.

### Exercise 45

**Voicing criticism**

In the last two paragraphs, underline the two sentences voicing criticism. Could you rephrase these criticisms more directly? Try to imagine what these journalists really think and voice their criticism without reproducing the text.

The press conference ended shortly afterwards and on his way back to the Swan Hotel (where his colleagues had been continuing with the interviews) David quickly grabbed a few sandwiches from the corner shop. To his great surprise, a blonde woman addressed him when he came out. "Chief Inspector David Rowe?" she asked with a smile. "Yes," David said. "I'm Cynthia Keefe from the society pages of the *Daily News*," the woman introduced herself. David felt that the term society pages sounded rather outdated[39] – but trust the *Daily News* to still have them! he thought. "What can I do for you?" he asked as politely as he could manage. He recognised the woman's voice as the voice of the reporter whose question, the day before at the actors' press conference, had upset Nora Palliser.

"Maybe we could do something for each other," Cynthia Keefe smiled. "In fact, I'd dearly like to help the police in my own way. At the press conference it was implied that the interests of the media and the requirements of the police do not always go together. I'm sure that our readers would

---

36 reproach: Vorwurf, Tadel  37 of the essence: wesentlich  38 to accommodate: (hier) entgegenkommen
39 outdated: unzeitgemäß

appreciate it if a young, and personable[40], policeman explained to them why the public sometimes has to wait for important information. Wouldn't you like to be able to tell your part of the story?"

Of all the bloody cheek[41], David thought. "You mean that you want to interview me?" he asked. "I didn't exactly think of an interview, it would be a human interest story, a nice long article with a number of photos," Cynthia Keefe was still smiling. "What makes you think that I'd be interested?" he asked, a bit more brusquely. "I'm sure that, as a policeman, you've long been dissatisfied with the bad press the police gets," the smile was still plastered on her face, "and that the public sees only the institution, not the people who are working day and night. Are you in a relationship[42]? We could also add a few quotes[43] from your wife or girlfriend, who I am sure is also concerned about …"

This was too much for David. "You forget that I did not give you an answer," he snapped, now barely able to conceal his disgust[44]. "I can assure you that neither I nor my girlfriend would be interested in the kind of story you have in mind." "Then how can I tempt[45] you? Do you need time to think it over? We're not without funds, you know … let me give you my card," Cynthia tried to slip[46] him her business card, but David did not take it. "I cannot think of any offer from the tabloids that might tempt me," he said disdainfully[47], "so please stop pestering me."

### Exercise 46

**Newspaper vocabulary**

In the last four paragraphs, find and underline the terms for

*1. Artikel – 2. Boulevardpresse – 3. die Rubrik „Gesellschaftliches" –*
*4. Geschichte aus dem Leben – 5. eine schlechte Presse bekommen – 6. Zitate*

The interviews at the Swan Hotel dragged on until late in the evening. Leo Sandys apologised for his emotional behaviour the day before. He had, it seemed, become quite friendly with Alan Gibson, whom he had met for the first time during rehearsals for the new TV series. To learn that Alan was not only dead but also the victim of a murder had been particularly distressing. Otherwise, he could not contribute much to the investigation.

---

40 personable: sympathisch und attraktiv  41 Of all the bloody cheek! (ugs.): Was für eine Frechheit!
42 relationship: (hier) feste Beziehung  43 quote: Zitat  44 disgust: Abscheu  45 to tempt: (ver)locken
46 to slip: zustecken  47 disdainful: verächtlich

Neither could location manager Emma Gill, who said that she had got to know Alan Gibson years before when she worked as a lowly[48] set designer's[49] assistant on a film called *The Fabulous Fraser Family*, "the copies of which are gathering dust somewhere," she said. "Alan sort of disappeared from sight a few ago," she remembered, "so it was nice to see him back in a quite important role." Jean Whyte also remembered hearing Alan Gibson and Kathy Cochrane discussing something. "They did raise their voices," she admitted, "but I have no idea what they were disagreeing about. It could have been anything. After weeks of filming we were all stressed out."

The interviews went on in this vein and David felt his concentration flag[50]. He was grateful that everything was being recorded and that Maud Johnstone still seemed to be on top of things. And he had not even found the time to phone Alix …

Exercise 47

### Phrasal verbs: Find the prepositions

In this chapter you might have found the phrasal verbs

1. *drag* _____
2. *figure* _____
3. *get* _____
4. *go* _____
5. *point* _____
6. *stop* _____
7. *tell* _____
8. *wake* _____

The German equivalents to these verbs are

*aufwachen – herausbekommen – hervorheben – rüffeln – sich hinziehen – vorbeischauen – zurückkehren – zusammenpassen*

Complete the phrasal verbs by adding their prepositions.

Emilia had spent the day in her agency's office. During her absence, her assistant Fiona had coped[51] admirably, but there were still things that she had to attend to personally[52]. Now Fiona had left – having taken the rest of the week off – and Emilia could no longer pretend that what was interesting her most right now was not Alan Gibson's murder. During the whole day she

---

48 lowly: klein und unbedeutend  49 set designer: Filmarchitekt, Bühnenbildner  50 to flag: nachlassen
51 to cope: die Lage meistern  52 to attend to personally: sich persönlich widmen

had thought about how best to start her own inquiries, and she had phoned Kathy Cochrane and arranged to have lunch with her the following day. In the late afternoon, she had had a look at the website of the East Yorkshire Police, where she had been able to watch a video of the press conference. She felt that David had handled the situation quite well – but it was to be hoped that the great interest of the media would not hamper[53] the work of the police.

She was about to leave when the doorbell announced a visitor. Half hoping that it would be David coming to talk, she buzzed[54] him in, and was amazed when she saw that the person coming up the stairs was Ivor Byrnes.

"Oh, Ivor, erm, good afternoon," she said, not able to hide her surprise. "You didn't expect me, did you?" Ivor answered. "No," Emilia replied, "how did you find me?" And why? she asked herself.

Ivor said nothing, but looked around, pensively. Emilia observed him. To her he seemed different. He was dressed differently, wearing an outdoor jacket and horn-rimmed glasses[55], and in his hand there were a woollen cap and a rolled-up newspaper. Maybe it's so he won't be recognised, she thought, now he looks almost normal. "Do you mind if I take this off?" Ivor asked, pointing to his jacket. "Not at all," Emilia said and got him a hanger[56] from the coat rack.

### Exercise 48

Frequently used phrases

Combine the verbs and nouns so that the two words together form a frequently used phrase. A look at the last few pages might help you.

1. to accommodate		a) one's surprise
2. to disappear		b) lunch
3. to gather		c) somebody's wishes
4. to give		d) one's voice
5. to have		e) from sight
6. to hide		f) dust
7. to raise		g) somebody ideas

---

53 to hamper: behindern  54 to buzz s.o. in: jmd. mit dem Türöffner hineinlassen  55 horn-rimmed glasses: Hornbrille  56 hanger: Bügel

"I was told that you are a private investigator," Ivor said at last. "When I'm not minding my partner's gallery, I am," she replied. "Some time ago, you and Robert Rutherford were involved in the recovery[57] of a painting that turned out to be by JMW Turner." "You've done your homework," Emilia said, looking at him questioningly. "I looked you up on the Internet today," he explained. "There's not very much about you there, but there was quite a bit about the painting." "I try to keep a low profile," Emilia explained, "St Stephen is not exactly London." "No," Ivor agreed.

"Well, I looked you up," he continued, "and then I remembered Charles Heyer, the vicar you brought to the party, and went to see him. He indicated that you have been involved in quite a number of cases that were … – how shall I put it? interesting?" Emilia had to smile. "At the very least," she said. "So you saw Charles – why? What can I do for you?"

"I should like to hire you," Ivor said. Emilia had not been wholly unprepared for this, but still … "Is this in connection with Alan's murder?" she asked. "Yes," he replied. "The police are investigating it," Emilia said. "I could hardly fail to notice," Ivor answered drily, "but they're going to have a hard job." "We hardly wear our personalities on our sleeves[58]," he explained after a pause. Emilia thought that he was right, but there had been other cases that, in the beginning, had looked difficult to solve. "Don't underestimate the police," she said – she owed David that much! – "It is not that I would not like to help, but it is still early days."

Ivor nodded. "You are right," he said, "but I feel that an insider who is already known to many of us, and who does not work for the police, by which I mean you, could prevent things from becoming more … entangled[59], more complicated than need be."

Emilia frowned. She did not quite know what to make of this – what had Charles told Ivor about her previous cases? and especially about her sometimes close cooperation with the very police detective who was now leading the investigation into Alan Gibson's murder? Was Ivor hoping to profit from such a relationship or were his motives more disinterested[60]? At the same time, she practically itched[61] to do something, and with Ivor Byrnes as her client she might get insights she otherwise would not.

Ivor sighed. "I wanted to show you this," he said, handing Emilia the newspaper he had brought. Emilia recognised the *Daily News*, which had

---

57 recovery: Wiederbeschaffung  58 to wear s.th. on one's sleeve: etw. sichtbar zur Schau stellen
59 entangled: verwickelt  60 disinterested: uneigennützig  61 to itch to do s.th.: darauf brennen, etw. zu tun

not made the death of Alan Gibson its lead story[62], but Nora Palliser's distress. Both the photos and the headline disgusted her. "That's tasteless," she said, "poor Nora." "I'm sure it's only the first of many," Ivor said. "We are more or less used to things like this, but I fear that this time, some of the tabloids are going to go over the top[63]. I've contacted my lawyer – there's not much we can do about this one. But if there is any way I can contribute to speeding up the investigation and to lessen Nora's distress …" "I see," Emilia said.

"Look," she then said, "I'll help you if I can. I cannot promise to do everything you ask of me. And if I think it fit to work with the police, I'll do it." Ivor gave her a long look, but then something in his face relaxed. "Fair enough[64]," he said.

### Exercise 49

Translate the phrases

Have another look at the frequently used phrases you found in Exercise 48. Translate them into German. Try to find phrases that are often used in the German language and compare them with the English phrases. Do you think that a one-to-one translation is possible?

When Ivor Byrnes had left, Emilia was elated[65] to be able to have a legitimate excuse to start her own investigation, but at the same time she was pensive. She understood Ivor's reasons for hiring her, but she did not feel that she knew her client at all. A call to Charles's mobile only resulted in his hurriedly and contritely[66] telling her that yes, Ivor had paid him a visit and that he was very sorry for not telling her about it at once, but he had had to leave for a parish council meeting[67], which was still ongoing, and would get back[68] to her asap.

So all Emilia was left with was to do what Ivor Byrnes had done: to look up her new client on the Internet. This produced an amazing number of results, and for the next hour and a half she trawled[69] celebrity[70] websites, fan pages dedicated[71] exclusively to the actor and a number of seemingly reputable Internet sources. She saw photos of Ivor Byrnes receiving his

---

62 lead story: Titelgeschichte  63 to go over the top: eine Grenze überschreiten  64 fair enough: (etwa) meinetwegen  65 elated: freudig erregt  66 contrite: reumütig  67 parish council meeting: Sitzung des Pfarrgemeinderats  68 to get back to s.o.: (hier) zurückrufen  69 to trawl: durchforsten  70 celebrity: Berühmtheit, Promi  71 dedicated: gewidmet

BAFTA award; together with James Riddell; accompanying a well-known actress to a charity function[72] (both looking gorgeous in dinner jacket[73] and evening gown); at the funeral of a good friend, next to the friend's widow (was it the death of this friend Nicholas Trent had alluded[74] to on the night of the party?); in the street with a pretty woman and a young child in a stroller[75] (the fan who had posted the photo was relieved to be able to say that these were his sister and nephew). All this did not really help Emilia in making out Ivor Byrnes's character, but she was sure that he had a complicated life.

Exercise 50

### Acronyms in spoken English

Even in spoken English some acronyms[76] are used. In the last two paragraphs you might have found the acronyms "asap" and "BAFTA", and in the following list there are further acronyms. What do they mean and how do you pronounce them?

*1.* aka – *2.* CV – *3.* DIY – *4.* FAQ – *5.* MP – *6.* SOCOs – *7.* TLC – *8.* WAG

---

72 charity function: Wohltätigkeitsveranstaltung  73 dinner jacket: Smoking  74 to allude: anspielen
75 stroller: Kinder-Sportwagen, Buggy  76 acronym: Akronym, Initialwort, das sich aus den Anfangsbuchstaben mehrerer Wörter zusammensetzt (wie UNO)

## Chapter 6

David's day began at the police station. There were a number of things to take care of, among them phone calls to London, where Maud Johnstone had travelled early in the morning. She was to have a closer look at the Hampstead flat of the murdered man, after a first inspection had been done by the Metropolitan Police[1]. Since Gibson had been living in London, the Met was looking after that end of things.

David would dearly have liked to go himself, not only to get more information about Alan Gibson by seeing the flat with his own eyes, but also to spend a bit of time with Alix. Whenever he could get away from work early, he took the express train from York, which reached London in a mere two hours. With the time he needed to get from St Stephen to York and from Liverpool Street Station to where Alix lived, it was still a four-hour journey and he usually had to leave early the next morning, but his crazy work schedule often only allowed these quick visits. Today, however, he had to be in court[2] later in the morning, to testify[3] in connection with another case. It couldn't be helped, but he also couldn't help to feel sorry for himself.

Alix. He had to find half an hour to phone her. In the last two days there had only been time for a number of hurried text messages[4]. She was very likely aware that he wouldn't be able to come this weekend, but even so he half longed to hear her voice and half dreaded to have to tell her that another long-anticipated[5] weekend together in London would come to nothing.

His telephone rang. "Emilia Ramsay to see you, sir," the desk sergeant[6] said. "Tell her to come up," David replied, asking himself what could be the matter. It was a bit early for Emilia to pay him a visit.

"I'm glad you're in," Emilia said, "I wasn't sure, but I did not want to tell you on the phone." "Some things are better done in person," David agreed. He wondered what she meant – but there was a look in her eyes he had seen before. "Wait …," he began. "Ivor Byrnes has asked me to look into Alan Gibson's murder and I've agreed," she quickly said.

---

1 Metropolitan Police (Met): die Londoner Polizei (Scotland Yard)  2 court: Gericht  3 to testify: eine Aussage machen  4 text message: SMS  5 long-anticipated: lang erwartet  6 desk sergeant: der diensthabende Polizist am Empfang eines Polizeireviers

## Getting around

Find arguments in favour of the means of transport (1 to 4) – and reasons why it might not be convenient to use them. Use the notes in the list to form sentences with the pros and cons[7].

*1. bike – 2. car – 3. train – 4. plane*

*congestion on the motorway – crowded carriages – eco-friendly and healthy – fear of flying – look at the landscape – oversea travel – transport of heavy items – wind and rain*

---

"Are you out of your mind[8]? This is a murder investigation," he protested. "And is it Ivor Byrnes's business? It's police business, I'd say." "Calm down, David," Emilia replied. "I do not intend to do anything that could hamper the police investigation. Or anything that could become dangerous." "Haven't I heard that before," he grumbled. Emilia raised her right eyebrow – in that typical way of hers – and then smiled a little ruefully[9]. "I suppose you have," she said.

"Ivor showed me a newspaper with photos of Nora and him on the front page," she explained, "I cannot even imagine how it must feel to be at the mercy[10] of the tabloids. He wants to help the investigation along – and I think it's a good idea. We might be able to find out things that the police cannot. And I'm going to share anything that might have a bearing on the investigation." David shook his head. "I still don't like it," he said, "but we've been through it all before."

"Have you found out anything yet?" Emilia inquired. "Not so very much," he conceded, adding, "It is early days, we're hardly through with interviewing all the people who attended the party. And they have told us surprisingly little, Ivor Byrnes being a case in point[11]!" "I can imagine," Emilia said. The way she said it made David realise that he had better not ask her to share information about Ivor as well – but that she would do it if she had to.

"Aren't you friends with Kathleen Cochrane?" he then asked, taking care to speak in a more normal voice. "Sort of[12]," Emilia said, "I've not

---

7 pros and cons: Vor- und Nachteile  8 out of one's mind: verrückt  9 rueful: reumütig, kleinlaut  10 at the mercy of s.o./s.th.: jmd./etw. ausgeliefert  11 case in point: ein typisches Beispiel  12 sort of (ugs.): irgendwie schon

known her long, but I know her well enough to have lunch with her." "When?" "Today," she replied. "You might want to ask Ms Cochrane about her discussion with Alan Gibson at the party and about how she got home," David said. He was amused to note that this time both of Emilia's eyebrows shot up. "You are incorrigible[13]," she said.

### Exercise 52

### Summarise[14] what has happened

Emilia tells Robert that she is helping to investigate the murder of Alan Gibson. Formulate a few sentences from Emilia's perspective, concerning what Ivor has asked her, what David thinks of it and concerning her lunch appointment with Kathy Cochrane.

---

Emilia and Kathy met at the King's Head, which in Emilia's opinion was one of the nicest pubs in St Stephen. The tourist season being long over, it was quite empty. They found a table in a window niche where the sun – the weather being unexpectedly fine for the end of November – warmed their backs, ordered their food at the bar and sat down to wait.

"How have you been?" Emilia asked. Kathy shrugged her shoulders. "As can be expected," she said, "not too bad, I suppose." But Emilia noticed that she looked out of spirits, which was, of course, understandable.

"The news of Alan's death came as quite a shock," Emilia said. "I did not know him at all well, but we had spent quite a lot of time in the same room. – Are you really alright? You do look pale, and you knew him much better than I did." "Oh, I'm alright," Kathy replied. "I only wish that I could think as well of him as I did some days ago." Emilia looked at her inquiringly. "What happened?" she asked. "I don't want to pry[15] …"

Kathy did not answer at once. "We quarrelled," she then said. "Quite late at the party. He made a pass at me and I refused. We had an unpleasant discussion." "Oh," Emilia said. "Actually, I thought that he tried the same thing with me. Something must have bugged[16] him that evening." "It might have been all the alcohol around," Kathy said, "you see, Alan was

---

13 incorrigible: unverbesserlich  14 to summarise: zusammenfassen  15 to pry: (übertrieben) neugierig sein  16 to bug s.o.: jmd. umtreiben

an alcoholic. He was dry, I believe, but he must have found the situation at the party very difficult."

"I didn't know that," Emilia replied. "I got the impression that he did not drink because he had to drive, but then he told me that he could always spend the night at the house …" "If he had only done that," Kathy replied.

### Exercise 53

### At the restaurant

There are some typical sentences you say when you're having a meal with others. But in each of the situations 1 to 3 you shouldn't use one of the sentences a to c (or b).

1. *Something you are about to eat seems to be very good.*

    a) *This reeks very good.* – b) *This smells lovely.* – c) *This looks delicious.*

2. *You are about to begin eating.*

    a) *Bon appétit!* – b) *Good appetite!*

3. *You want to pay for the meals of everyone present.*

    a) *I would like to invite you.* – b) *This is on me.* – c) *Let me get this.*


"Where did you stay that night?" Emilia inquired. "I didn't want to stay at the house," Kathy explained. "I feared that Alan would make a nuisance of himself[17]. I left in my car, but nearly hit a dry stone wall – too much wine, I'm afraid. So I parked somewhere off the road and kipped[18] on the back seat for an hour or two. It took me very long to get back to the hotel, which the police think mightily[19] strange." "Oh," Emilia said with feeling. "I might have done the same," she added.

"Try to tell the police inspector that," Kathy replied. "Have you talked to him?" she asked. "Yes," Emilia said, "he asked lots of questions about the party." "Did you tell him about the pass Alan made at you?" "No …" "Couldn't you do it? It might make my story appear more believable. Do you know the inspector, I mean, you being a private investigator?"

---

17 to make a nuisance of oneself: andere belästigen  18 to kip (ugs.): pennen  19 mightily (ugs.): überaus (ironisch)

"I've worked with Inspector Rowe," Emilia said carefully, "and of course I can tell him." "He was determined to find inconsistencies[20] in what I told him," Kathy complained. "How do *you* get along with him?" "We've had our differences," Emilia replied neutrally, "but it has all worked out somehow. Try not to worry too much. Inspector Rowe is really not so very unreasonable[21]. The police have to ask all those questions."

### Exercise 54

**What's wrong?**

Have another look at Exercise 53. What is wrong with the sentences you shouldn't have used?

They were signalled that their food was ready, and while they were eating spoke about what was happening at the hotel. Kathy, however, was rather reticent[22] about it. She attempted a joke about them all sleeping a lot, but then admitted that some people were bored and that speculation about what could have happened to Alan was rife[23]. "It's unpleasant," she said, "if there only was something that could help the investigation! I believe I would be the first to pass on the information." She was clearly rattled[24] at having been grilled[25] by the police.

"You said you were sorry that you and Alan parted on bad terms[26]," Emilia remembered. "Was it really that bad? He must have realised that he wasn't exactly on his best behaviour." "Maybe," Kathy said, "but the problem is that I always thought I knew people, and now I don't believe that that is true." "What do you mean?" Emilia really wondered what Kathy wanted to say. "It's doesn't matter," Kathy merely replied, "I'm simply sad about what happened, I suppose." Emilia realised that there was nothing to be gained from pressing[27] Kathy further. But she felt that there was something that the other woman did not want to tell her.

"Are you going to go back to the hotel?" Emilia asked after a while. "No, I've got some work to do, fortunately" Kathy replied. "I'm off to Rosedale Hall, where we're filming next. There are some loose ends from preproduction to tie up[28] and Christopher and I are quite happy to do it."

20 inconsistency: Ungereimtheit  21 unreasonable: uneinsichtig  22 reticent: zurückhaltend  23 speculation is rife: Mutmaßungen grassieren  24 rattled: verunsichert  25 grilled: (hier) in die Mangel genommen, ausgefragt  26 to part on bad terms: im Streit auseinandergehen  27 to press: bedrängen  28 to tie up loose ends: noch offene Fragen/Probleme klären

## Exercise 55

### Phases of film production

Note which activities belong to the preproduction (1), the filming (2) and the postproduction (3) phase of filmmaking.

*a) call sheets are handed out – b) camera operators are at work – c) caterers prepare food – d) colours are corrected – e) film footage is produced – f) locations are selected – g) make-up artists are busy – h) scenes are repeated – i) sets are designed – j) sound mixing is done – k) special effects are generated – l) the actors are cast – m) the film crew are hired – n) the film is edited – o) the production schedule is amended constantly – p) the production schedule is drawn up – q) the script is written – r) the soundtrack is synchronised with the images*

David, after giving his statement in court, returned to the police station. There was nothing from Maud yet, so he decided to call Alix. He did not usually phone her at work, but, his work schedule being so unpredictable[29], he hoped that she would be able to talk for a bit.

Alix wanted to know about his current[30] case and _____ (1) they spoke about that. "There were some snippets of the press conference on the TV yesterday," she said, "it was lovely to see you, but not nearly enough …" "There's been _____ (2) media interest," David replied. He did not tell her about the questionable[31] offer he had got from the *Daily News* journalist – it had been unpleasant and he refused to waste his precious time on the phone with Alix by dwelling[32] on it.

"I can imagine," Alix said. "It's the favourite topic[33] of some of the nurses and doctors here as well. They're _____ (3) fans of Ivor Byrnes. I've impressed on anyone you've met not to let slip[34] that you're investigating the case! There would be no end of questions!" "You might be able to take a few days of compassionate leave[35] then," he replied. "I only hope that there will be some progress soon. So far, we've not been very _____ (4) …"

29 unpredictable: unberechenbar  30 current: derzeitig  31 questionable: fragwürdig  32 to dwell on s.th.: sich (unnötig lange) mit etw. aufhalten  33 topic: (Gesprächs)thema  34 to let slip: ausplaudern  35 compassionate leave: Urlaub wegen eines privaten Problems

### Exercise 56

Find the appropriate words …

… for the gaps in the two paragraphs on page 73. Which words from the following groups are appropriate, which are not?

1. *for a short time – briefly – curtly – concisely*
2. *quite a bit of – extensive – a great deal of – pretty much*
3. *avid – large – tall – great*
4. *lucky – successful – fruitful – succeeding*

---

He briefly told her about the interviews with the actors. "Only a short time ago, we were talking about Ivor Byrnes and Nora Palliser at Emilia and Robert's, and now you're talking to them in connection with a murder," Alix said. "Emilia tells me that Ivor is not very communicative and that Nora is simply lovely." "So you've spoken to Emilia," David replied, "I'm sure that she can tell you much more about them than I can." He was glad to leave it at that.

"Darling, about this weekend …," he began. "You won't be able to make it," she stated, matter-of-factly, but not able to hide her disappointment. "No," he said softly. "I'm sure that I'll find something to do," Alix said, "but I'm a bit concerned about, well, you know …" "I know," David only replied. There were so many things he wanted to say. He was grateful that she did not add to his stress by always pointing out that he should take it easier, but theirs was a difficult situation and he often racked his brains[36] about it. "I am …," he began and then saw that Maud was trying to phone him on his landline. "I have to stop," he said, "Maud is calling. She went to Gibson's flat and might have some news." "I see," Alix sighed, "and I have to be somewhere else as well." "I miss you," he said, and after a few goodbye sentences they ended the call.

"I'm still at the flat," Maud said, "and it's interesting." "That's good news," David said. "The first thing," she explained," is that it's a nice two-bedroom[37] flat in Hampstead, quiet, but near the tube station." "Must have

---

36 to rack one's brains: sich den Kopf zerbrechen  37 two-bedroom: mit zwei Schlafzimmern (meistens eine Dreizimmerwohnung)

been expensive," he assumed. "Alan Gibson rented it, but yes, it is expensive. We found the contract, Gibson paid his landlord 695 pounds per week. The interesting thing is that he moved in two years ago, at a time when, if I remember correctly, he was rather down on his luck[38]." "Could he have had some savings? Some other kind of income?"

### Exercise 57

Telephone conversations

Complete the lines below by inserting the appropriate questions or statements.

1. _____ – Who may I say is calling?

2. _____ Hold the line, please.

3. _____ Would you like to leave a message?

4. I'm afraid that she's not in at the moment. _____

5. _____ The line is very bad.

6. Would you ask her to call me back? – Yes, of course.
   _____

a) Can I take a message?

b) Could I have your phone number, please?

c) I cannot understand what you're saying.

d) May I speak to Ms Hill, please?

e) I'm putting you through.

f) The line's engaged.


Maud gave a short laugh. "The latter," she said. "We also found his _____ (Kontoauszüge)." "Didn't we have a look at them yesterday?" "What we requested were the statements of the bank that

[38] do be down on one's luck: vom Glück verlassen sein

issued his _____ (Scheckkarte). Alan Gibson, however, had several _____ (Konten). We might have learned of this eventually, but it's a good thing that we found the statements now. Because this is where it gets really interesting."

"You're keeping me in suspense[39]," David said. "I think," Maud continued, "that Alan Gibson used the bank account we knew of for official purposes and the other accounts, some of them _____ (Konten im Ausland), to spread money. These funds were not _____ (überwiesen) from another account, but were mainly _____ (Bareinzahlungen). I won't go into details now, but I do not think that the _____ (Finanzamt) would easily have got wind of it. For the last years, Mr Gibson has been enjoying a nice little income." "That's interesting indeed," David said.

### Exercise 58

**Some banking terms**

Complete the two paragraphs above with the words

*bank account – bank statements – cash deposit – debit card – inland revenue – offshore account – to transfer*

"And that's not all we found," Maud continued triumphantly. "We also found a diary[40] for 2010, with a number of self-explanatory[41] and some more mysterious notes. We've been comparing the dates of the cash deposits with the notes in the agenda and there seem to be a number of links. Some of the corresponding notes are words that obviously refer to something that we cannot make sense of yet, but others are two capital letters[42]. For example we found the letters AD on June 7, the same day that cash deposits of 5,000 pounds each were made to two bank accounts." "It seems to be a private sort of bookkeeping. Could they be initials or some sort of code?" "The former, I think," Maud paused dramatically. "You see, on August 28 and on October 4, 2010, there are deposits of 9,000 pounds each and in the corresponding days of the agenda there are the letters IB. Ring any bells[43]?" "It certainly does," David said.

[39] to keep s.o. in suspense: jmd. auf die Folter spannen  [40] diary: (hier) Taschenkalender  [41] self-explanatory: selbsterklärend  [42] capital letter: Großbuchstabe  [43] ring any bells?: klingelt's da nicht bei dir?

"How long will it take you to obtain bank statement information about a potential suspect?" David, only minutes later, asked Brian Morris, who at the police station often dealt with requests like these. "How soon do you need it?" Brian asked. "It's in connection with the murder of Alan Gibson," David replied, "so as soon as possible?" "I have to follow procedures[44], but if we're in luck, I can get it more or less at once. Give me the name and the time in question," Brian said. "The relevant months are August and October 2010, and the name is Ivor Byrnes." Brian gave a whistle[45] of surprise. "Oh boy," he said.

### Exercise 59

### Idioms with "some" and "any"

Complete the following idioms with "some" or "any". What do they mean?

1. Ring _____ bells?
2. _____ Tom, Dick or Harry
3. Do not lose _____ sleep over it.
4. to do _____ straight talking
5. You win _____, you lose _____.
6. to have _____ merit
7. You've got _____ nerve!
8. Don't get _____ ideas!

### Exercise 60

### English idioms – German idioms

Have another look at Exercise 59 and try to find German translations for the completed idioms that are also idioms. Are they word-by-word translations of the English idioms?

---

44 to follow procedures: den offiziellen Weg gehen  45 whistle: Pfiff

# Chapter 7

Ivor Byrnes did not answer his mobile phone, which made David uneasy. Where could he be? David decided to have a look at where the actor was staying near Moreton, an additional, and not unimportant, reason being that he had not yet managed to see the house where the party had taken place.

Brian Morris had managed to get hold of Ivor Byrnes's bank statements admirably quickly and the evidence[1] was there: Shortly before August 28, 2010, Ivor Byrnes had withdrawn[2] 20,000 pounds from his account, and shortly before October 4, the same sum had been taken out. The actor seemed to be able to afford it and, from what David could see, spent quite a lot of money, but the two cash withdrawals stuck out[3]. Ivor Byrnes had some explaining to do.

David arrived at the house, which, for a holiday home, he thought very grand indeed, and rang the bell. Nicholas Trent answered the door. He was obviously surprised to see David, but pleasantly invited him to come in.

David explained that he was looking for Ivor Byrnes and would like to have a look at the rooms the party had taken place in. "I don't know where Ivor is, I'm afraid," Nicholas replied, "but feel free to wander around." "Do you need to see the bedrooms?" he added, a bit apprehensively[4], and was relieved when David assured him that the reception rooms[5] would do.

Nicholas then excused himself, saying that he had something to do in the kitchen, and David spent the next five minutes alone. It was a lovely house, he thought, but needed to be filled with people. It was to be hoped that not every party would bring about the results the previous one had.

### Exercise 61

Rephrase the sentences

Underline the sentences (or parts of sentences) in the two paragraphs above that use reported speech. Rephrase them using direct speech (or thought).

---

1 evidence: Beweis, Beleg  2 to withdraw: abheben  3 to stick out: hervorstechen, auffallen  4 apprehensive: besorgt  5 reception rooms: die Räume eines Hauses, in denen Gäste empfangen werden

He joined Nicholas in the well-appointed[6] kitchen, where Jessica Sleightholme, headphones in her ears, sat flipping[7] through a glossy magazine[8]. "I'm making lunch," Nicholas explained. David only nodded. He realised that he was hungry, but a glimpse towards the mess around the cooker did not make him wish for an invitation.

"I hope you haven't been pestered by the media," he said to Nicholas, waiting for Jessica to realise that he was there. Maybe she knew about Ivor's whereabouts[9]. "Luckily they've not discovered us yet," Nicholas replied. "They seem to be under the impression that we're all staying at the Swan," Jessica, who had taken off her headphones, added. "I suppose we should be grateful the police didn't make public that Alan met his death after the party here. If the journos[10] figure out where we are, I'll be in touch with a security service at once."

"Jessica, do you know where Ivor is?" Nicholas asked. Jessica frowned. "He's not here. He might be at the Hotel," she said, "he seems to think it a good idea to show his face there every now and then." "Maybe he is simply getting bored here," Nicholas pointed out, "or he doesn't want to disturb the domestic bliss[11] of Miss Bennet and Mr Bingley." "Not that they're making much of a success of it," he mumbled under his breath[12]. Jessica shot Nicholas a disdainful look and rolled her eyes at David, who decided that it was time to leave.

Exercise 62

### Nonverbal communication

Complete the sentences 1 to 6 by inserting an appropriate form of:

*to nod – to raise an eyebrow – to roll one's eyes – to shake one's head – to shrug one's shoulders – to wink*

1. To answer in the negative, you _____.

2. You _____ to affirm something – or to acknowledge someone you meet.

3. To signal a number of things like astonishment, mild disapproval or amusement, you can _____.

---

6 well-appointed: gut ausgestattet  7 to flip through: durchblättern  8 glossy magazine: Hochglanzzeitschrift
9 whereabouts: Aufenthaltsort  10 journo (ugs.): kurz für Journalist  11 domestic bliss: häusliches Glück
12 under one's breath: leise, im Flüsterton

4. If someone annoys or frustrates you, you sometimes cannot help
   _____.

5. Some things should not be taken so very seriously – you might signal this by _____ at somebody.

6. If you _____, you might want to show your indifference.

At the Swan Hotel, it wasn't easy to find anybody. The public rooms where people had gathered the day before were empty. David thought that, after a day of waiting to be interviewed by the police and speculating about what could have happened, many must have wanted to get outside and would be taking advantage[13] of the sunny weather. The reception was unmanned[14], but he could see that there weren't many keys missing. Everybody seemed to have flown out. He went up the stairs, to the room where Jacob Francis had worked the day before, and was in luck: Jacob was in – but he hadn't seen Ivor Byrnes either. "The *Daily News* have been busy again," once more he handed David a copy of the newspaper, "they seem to home in[15] on Ivor and Nora." "A real-life Mr and Mrs Darcy?" the headline said, once again showing photos of Ivor and Nora, which, however, seemed to be publicity photos. "It's not as offensive as yesterday," David said, "maybe they're running out of steam[16]." "Let's hope so," Jacob sighed, "but somehow I can't help wondering what they'll come up with next."

### Exercise 63

#### Booking hotel accommodation[17]

You are on the phone making a hotel booking. Formulate the (short) questions you are likely to ask concerning the topics:

1. vacancies for the following weekend – 2. double room with twin beds[18] – 3. ensuite[19] bathroom – 4. wifi network – 5. room rate – 6. special rate if you stay three nights – 7. check in and check out time – 8. confirmation of booking

---

13 to take advantage of s.th.: sich etw. zunutze machen  14 unmanned: unbesetzt  15 to home in on s.o.: sich auf jmd. einschießen  16 to run out of steam: an Schwung einbüßen, das Interesse verlieren
17 accommodation: Unterkunft  18 twin beds: zwei Einzelbetten im Doppelzimmer  19 ensuite: mit eigenem Bad

David left the room. He was not in the best of moods – the police might finally have a lead, but everything *he* did was not exactly productive. He was hungry, had not slept enough for some time and speaking to Alix on the phone had only added to his general frustration. He was making his way towards the hotel's lobby when a door opened and out came – Nora Palliser. She turned around and, recognising David, her serious expression changed into a smile.

"Hi," she said. "Hello," David replied. "I thought there was nobody here." "We've been getting on each others' nerves a bit," Nora explained, "so most of us have gone out, I believe. The weather is so nice. I only returned a few minutes ago." "And you're leaving again?" "I was going to have a bite to eat," she said. "They're doing lunch specials[20] at the restaurant downstairs, for people to eat during their lunch break." She looked at David. "You wouldn't care to join me?" she asked hesitatingly, "But I forget, you won't have the time." "Actually, I was just thinking about where to have a spot[21] of lunch," David replied quickly.

### Exercise 64

### Frequently used phrases

Combine the verbs and the nouns (or noun phrases) so that the words together form a frequently used phrase. A look at the last few pages might help you.

1. to be          a) on each other's nerves
2. to come up   b) out of steam
3. to have       c) with an idea
4. to run        d) a bite to eat
5. to show       e) in luck
6. to get        f) one's face

"I should go out to eat more often," he said a few minutes later when they were sitting in the hotel's rather nice dining room, its French windows

20 lunch special: günstiges Mittagessen  21 a spot of (ugs.): ein bisschen

affording[22] a view on a small sunny garden. "What do you usually do?" Nora wanted to know. "There is a sort of canteen at the police station," he said, "which you do not want to hear about." "No, I don't," she laughed, adding, "I used[23] to work in a school kitchen, a couple of years ago, when I did not make much money acting."

Nora was easy to talk _____ (1), and David was glad that she did not think it necessary to talk _____ (2) Alan Gibson's death. He decided to save any questions he might have _____ (3) later – it was so good to have some respite _____ (4) all the things that were bothering him! The minutes flew, _____ (5) them speaking _____ (6) Nora's career and _____ (7) St Stephen and its scenic[24] surroundings[25], which David admitted had taken him some time to truly appreciate. "Actually, I'm going _____ (8) a short walk this afternoon, followed _____ (9) a cup of tea with …" Nora looked _____ (10) her watch and gave small yelp[26] of surprise. "Excuse me, David, I've got to make a quick phone call." She got _____ (11) her mobile _____ (12) her bag and scrolled _____ (13) a number. "Emilia?" she asked, "are you _____ (14) your way already? … oh, good … look, could you pick me _____ (15) a bit later? I'm just finishing lunch and I need to go _____ (16) my room and change[27], would half past be alright? … Great, I'll see you then." David had to suppress a grin. Trust Emilia not to lose any time!

### Exercise 65

#### Prepositions

In a conversation, it is sometimes difficult to find the correct preposition. To practice, complete the text above with the prepositions

*about (3x) – at – by – for (2x) – from (2x) – on – out – to (3x) – up – with*

"I'd love to have coffee with you," Nora said, regret in her voice, "but I'm going for a walk with Emilia, Emilia Ramsay. She works at the gallery we've been filming at. You will have met her!" David mind raced – it was clear that

22 to afford s.th.: (hier) etw. bieten  23 used to do s.th.: etw. früher getan haben  24 scenic: landschaftlich reizvoll  25 surroundings: Umgebung  26 yelp: Aufschrei  27 to change: sich umziehen

Nora did not know that Emilia was a private investigator – and his confusion must have shown on his face.

"She was at the party," Nora explained, "didn't you speak to her?" "I'm sure we did," David said, adding, "we spoke to about forty people and I couldn't be present at all the interviews."

"What are you doing now?" Nora wanted to know. "Going back to the station," David said, "I've been trying to get hold of Mr Byrnes, but haven't been able to find him." Nora looked at him curiously. "Ivor?" she asked. "We spoke on the phone this morning, and he said that he would be at Rosedale Hall. We're going to shoot the Pemberley scenes there. Some pre-production things need to be checked or changed, and he was going to lend Christopher and Kathy a hand." She hesitated. "Why do you need to speak to him?" she asked.

"We're still trying to learn as much about Alan Gibson as possible and he might be able to help with something," David said non-committally[28]. He was glad to know where he would find Ivor. With the media around, it was awkward to ask anyone to come to the police station and he wouldn't have to go all the way back to Moreton – Rosedale Hall was only five miles from St Stephen.

Exercise 66

Answer the questions

You don't need to put your answers in writing – try to practise your spoken English! (Suggestions for answers can be found in the key to the exercises.)

1. Why does David go to the house the actors have rented?
2. Why is he glad to have lunch with Nora?
3. Why is he glad to be able to find Ivor Byrnes at Rosedale Hall?

When they left the dining room, Nora did not go up the stairs. She had obviously decided to accompany David to the car park exit. "I'm sorry you

28 non-committally: unverbindlich

had to stay here in St Stephen," David said. "I understand that you were all to take a break, which I'm sure would have been well earned."

Nora shrugged her shoulders. "It doesn't matter much," she said. "It would have been nice to be home for a few days, but I'd only have caught up on sleep, which I can do here as well." "Ah, to catch up on lost sleep …," David said. "You look tired yourself," Nora said. "I am," David admitted. "How do *you* reconcile[29] your job with your private life?" she inquired, her voice full of sympathetic[30] interest, and for some moments David debated with himself how to answer the question. "It is not easy," he finally replied.

They went through the door and stopped. "Good-bye," David said, "I really enjoyed our lunch." "Maybe we'll see each other," Nora said softly, "good luck with the investigation." She made as if to go, but then hesitated and took a step towards David and the next thing he knew was that they were hugging[31] and he realised that Nora did hugs properly. Another thing he realised was that it felt rather nice to have her in his arms.

What was that? he asked himself a few minutes later, in his car. He hoped that Nora wouldn't make too much of it, it could cause no end of complications. As for himself, he had to admit that he was flattered[32] and that there certainly was some attraction. But there were many kinds of attraction … and what part of it was due to him feeling rather lonely sometimes? The situation with Alix in London and him in a job that required a lot of overtime[33] was difficult. Did this make him susceptible[34]? He had to find a solution, seriously had to think about it, he told himself, but now was not the right time. There was work to be done. So David tried to focus all of his attention on the traffic a town the size of St Stephen had to offer.

### Exercise 67

**More ways of nonverbal communication**

When do you (more than one answer may be possible)

*1. embrace – 2. hug – 3. give a kiss on the cheek – 4. shake hands – 5. squeeze someone's shoulder?*

*a) when you meet a business acquaintance*

*b) when you say hello or good-bye to a friend (especially if you're a woman)*

---

29 to reconcile: vereinbaren  30 sympathetic: einfühlsam  31 to hug: umarmen  32 flattered: geschmeichelt
33 overtime: Überstunden  34 susceptible: anfällig

*c)* when you seal an agreement

*d)* when you want to show someone that you sympathize with his difficult situation

*e)* when you want to show that you follow the principles of good sportsmanship

*f)* when you want to signal friendship or affection

*g)* when you want to signal friendship or affection more intimately

Rosedale Hall was a large and beautiful stone building in a dale[35] framed[36] by two ridges of hills[37]. It dated from Jacobean times, when the gardens, which were now the main attraction of the place, had also been first laid out. David had been at Rosedale before, on a case, and wanted to know how Simon Harding, the owner, was doing. But a young woman who worked for Simon told him that he was in London.

David then went to look for Ivor Byrnes. There were a number of people about. He saw Christopher Cox with a man he thought was the production designer and others, who were taking photos or measuring something, but not the man he was looking for. "Ivor? He was here an hour ago," or "he must be somewhere," were the answers David got.

He went out into the gardens, but, knowing that it would take ages to search them, turned back after a few minutes and returned inside. Finally he went up the grand staircase, and on the first floor, in a windowed recess[38], he saw Ivor Byrnes's back. He and Kathleen Cochrane seemed engaged in earnest conversation. When they heard David, they hastily turned round.

Neither was pleased to see him, but it couldn't be helped. "I'd like a word with Mr Byrnes," David said. "Alone." "Can't this wait?" Ivor asked, barely polite. "I'm afraid not," David replied sharply, "I had to come here because you didn't answer your phone." "And where do you want to talk?" Ivor asked. "Here will do," David replied, "unless you'd rather come to the police station." Ivor sighed. "We'll talk later," he said to Kathy.

35 dale: Tal (in Nordengland)  36 framed: gerahmt  37 ridge of hills: Hügelkette  38 windowed recess: Fensternische

"Are you sure that you gave us all the relevant facts about your relationship with Mr Gibson?" was David's first question. Ivor's face was inscrutable when he answered, "Absolutely sure." "Then how do you explain that you made two cash withdrawals of 20,000 pounds from your account on August 25 and October 2, 2010?" Ivor hesitated. "I gave the money to a fellow actor who had fallen on hard times[39]," he replied. "And Alan Gibson was the fellow actor?" David asked. Ivor sighed. "You seem to know about it," he replied. "Yes, he was. How did you learn that?"

David outlined what Maud Johnstone and their London colleagues had found out. "Nothing that you said yesterday," he concluded, "led me to believe that Alan Gibson and you were friends. So am I wrong in presuming that you did not give him the money for philanthropic reasons[40]?"

Ivor was silent for a whole minute and David felt that he was thinking about how best to tell his story. "He asked for the money urgently," Ivor said. "I do not doubt that," David replied, "but the question is, what did he give in return." "I think that you were being blackmailed[41]," he added, when no further answer seemed to come forward.

Ivor looked out of the window. "I have to protect my private life," he finally said, "and I cannot be too careful. Can you guarantee that nothing I'm going to tell you now will be known in public?" "I can guarantee no such thing," David replied, "but I do give you my word that nothing will get out that is not relevant to the case." Ivor pondered[42] this. "I see that that will have to be enough," he finally said.

"My best friend was Jeremy Froy," Ivor began, "he also was an actor, a well-known one. He died from cancer two years ago, and it took him a long time to die. I was often with him, as was Jeremy's wife, Beth. So Beth and I were thrown in each other's company and we …," again Ivor was silent, "we consoled each other … It would have hurt Jeremy, had he known, and not many people would have understood." He looked at David. "You were lovers," David stated. "We were," Ivor admitted, "I do not think we were in love, but it was an extraordinary situation. We were both lonely and distraught, and so it happened."

"Alan must have learned about it. We were mostly in Wiltshire, where Beth and Jeremy were living, but for a long time Jeremy, until he became too weak, went to London for medical treatments. Beth and I were careful,

---

39 to fall on hard times: eine Durststrecke haben  40 for philanthropic reasons: aus Menschenfreundlichkeit
41 to blackmail: erpressen  42 to ponder s.th: eingehend über etw. nachdenken

but we sometimes had to get out of the house. We took long walks, and I suppose that anyone could have followed us, if he had set his mind[43] to it. It seems that Alan had and that he took photos of us. He showed me one, of Beth and me in some street, I don't remember exactly where and it does not matter … If a photo like that had been given to a newspaper, I'd have had a hard time explaining what I was doing kissing my dying friend's wife. Jeremy would, of course, have been devastated, as Beth would have been. She was extremely vulnerable at that time." Ivor was silent.

Exercise 68

### Translate

1. Ivor Byrnes hat zweimal große Geldsummen von seinem Bankkonto abgehoben.

2. Emilia und Nora nutzten das gute Wetter und gingen spazieren.

3. Früher arbeitete Nora in einer Schulküche. Heute ist sie eine bekannte Schauspielerin.

David hardly knew what to say. But he understood how everything had happened. "I see," he eventually replied. "So Mr Gibson blackmailed you. Would you tell me about it?" "I suppose you could call it blackmail," Ivor said slowly, "but it was subtly[44] done. Alan and I were actors in the same film, he had a minor role[45] and I a much bigger one. The film was shot in a London studio, and Beth sometimes picked me up there. That was at the time when she and Jeremy still came to London. Some time later, when Jeremy was much worse, Alan first told me that he had noticed my close relationship with her and that he understood the difficulty of the situation. I asked him what the hell he meant. Alan just smiled and handed me the photo. He understood that we had to be careful who knew about it, he said."

"An hour or two later, he asked me if I could help him out moneywise[46]. I bluntly[47] asked him if he expected a payment for not telling anyone about me and Beth, but he merely smiled. He was sorry if I saw it that way, he

43 to set one's mind to s.th.: sich etw. in den Kopf setzen  44 subtle: (hier) raffiniert  45 minor role: (unwichtige) Nebenrolle  46 moneywise: was Geld betrifft  47 blunt: unverblümt

said, but that he was desperate. He owed money and the people who had lent it to him were running out of patience[48]." "And so you paid him – how much?" "I paid 20,000 pounds, twice," Ivor said. "He blackmailed you a second time?" "Yes, he did. Jeremy was dead then and I made it clear that this was the last time he would get any money from me." "He didn't try a third time?" "No," Ivor said. "I see what you're driving at[49]," he added fiercely[50], "but no, he didn't try for a third time."

"We found this private bookkeeping in Mr Gibson's flat," David said. "What is interesting is that the money we connected with your name, money Mr Gibson transferred to his own account, was only about half of the money you said you gave him." "I cannot help you there," Ivor replied. "Alan said that he had to repay debts. He might have needed the rest of the money for that or he might have spent it." "He might indeed," David said.

"Did Mr Gibson give you one of the photos?" David then asked. "I did not want them and tore them to shreds before his eyes," Ivor said. "There will have been other copies anyway." "Have you told anyone about being blackmailed by Mr Gibson?" was David's next question. Ivor shook his head. "Not even Mrs Froy?" "Especially not Mrs Froy," Ivor insisted. "Do you think that Mrs Froy would be prepared to make a statement about what you've just told me about your relationship?" "I'd hate to ask that of her," Ivor replied, "I think that yes, she would. But I'd really like to avoid it."

David thought. "Let's see if we need her statement," he said. "What we do need, however, is a statement from you. I have to ask you to accompany me to the police station. We're going to be very discreet, but we need to put this in writing. And I have to ask you not to leave St Stephen for the time being."

"You have to pursue[51] this, don't you?" Ivor asked. "We do," David said.

### Exercise 69

#### Question tags

Question tags (Frageanhängsel) are frequently used in spoken English. In German, you would simply say something like "nicht wahr?", but English questions tags are more complex and refer to the verb and subject in the main sentence. Complete the following questions by using question tags.

---

48 to run out of patience: die Geduld verlieren  49 to drive at s.th.: auf etw. anspielen  50 fierce: grimmig
51 to pursue: (weiter)verfolgen

1. *You have to pursue this, _____?*
2. *You gave the money to Alan Gibson, _____?*
3. *Mr Gibson didn't blackmail you a third time, _____?*
4. *You haven't given him any money since the second time, _____?*
5. *You cannot help me here, _____?*
6. *There will have been other copies of the photo anyway, _____?*
7. *You aren't prepared to speak to Mrs Froy about this, _____?*
8. *You won't be leaving St Stephen, _____?*

Emilia's day ended in a pub called The Green Man. When she and Nora had returned from their walk they had had tea in the tearoom opposite the Swan Hotel, where they had met Leo Sandys and his girlfriend Audrey, who had come up from London to keep Leo company. Leo and Audrey had expressed an interest in checking out St Stephen's pub scene and Emilia was only too pleased to show them some of the town's nicer pubs.

So they met at eight – Emilia, Leo and Audrey as well as Jean Whyte and Christopher Cox, who tagged along[52], and visited the King's Head, the Witch and Fairy and, finally, The Green Man.

Everyone's mood was rather more sombre[53] than would have been usual for a pub crawl[54]. But, as Jean put[55] it, "it wouldn't have been any good to get drunk alone in one's room," and so (unfortunately, Emilia thought) everyone made an effort to briefly forget about the sad death of Alan Gibson.

Still, it turned out to be an interesting evening. Emilia learned a lot about the difficulties of becoming an actor and of finding a job in the film industry. "We've all landed on our feet[56], for the time being, at least," Leo said. "But I spent a good part of last year doing TV commercials[57]. I always

---

52 to tag along: sich anschließen  53 sombre: trüb, düster  54 pub crawl: Zug durch die Kneipen  55 to put s.th.: (hier) etw. ausdrücken  56 to land on one's feet: auf die Beine kommen, sich etablieren  57 commercial: Werbespot

expect some journalist to write that I'm playing George Wickham, but am much better known for being the guy who tries out the beds in the commercials of some furniture chain[58]." "You probably are," Audrey remarked, "but that is going to change very soon."

Christopher confided that he had always wanted to study film, but had not managed to get a place. "I began to study English literature instead," he explained, "and spent all my free time doing unpaid work. My first paid job was as production assistant on a film called *The Fabulous Fraser Family*. It fell to me to organise accommodation for all the actors. Afterwards I really thought about a career change. I'd have been eminently suited[59] to the diplomatic service …" Everyone had to laugh.

"You and Kathy have been doing a great job at keeping everyone happy," Emilia said. "But not everyone was happy on Monday night," Jean replied sadly. There was a short silence. "So it seems," Christopher sighed.

### Exercise 70

### Pub culture

Complete the sentences below, using the words

*darts – gastropub – pool – pub crawl – pub grub – pub quizzes – publican – regulars – village pub*

1. The _____ is often the heart of a small local community, while the many public houses of a bigger place invite you to do a _____.

2. The people who haunt the local pub are called _____, and the pub landlord is also called _____.

3. A _____ concentrates on serving quality food, while in many pubs you get simple meals that are also referred to as _____.

4. Some pubs hold _____, which are a great way to meet the locals. Another way to spend time in a pub is to play _____ or _____.

---

58 furniture chain: Möbelkette  59 eminently suited: bestens geeignet

# Chapter 8

On Friday, David arrived at work late. After he had taken Ivor Byrnes's statement, he and Maud, who had returned from London, had tried to make sense of the less obvious annotations[1] in Alan Gibson's diary, of which Maud had brought photocopies. It had been very late when he got home and that morning he had slept through his alarm clock.

When he entered the station he had the feeling of being looked at oddly, but put it down[2] to still being very tired. He went to his office, put coffee into the coffee maker, took his mobile out of the pocket of his sports jacket[3] and had begun to get the papers on his desk in an order that would allow him to work with them, when Maud came into the room. She had a newspaper in her hand. "You need to see this," she said, in a voice that was hovering[4] between confusion and compassion.

It was the *Daily News*, once again, David thought. But when he had a look at the front page, he thought that his heart would stop. There was another photo of Nora – and himself, hugging in the door of the Swan Hotel! "Is Darcy's first name David?" the headline read. "Nora Palliser in passionate embrace[5] with handsome policeman David Rowe."

David sat down in his chair, trying to breathe regularly, and then scanned the article below. He did not want to read it, but he had to. He caught only parts of what was said – "car park of the Swan Hotel in St Stephen, where Nora is staying", "one of the more creative investigation techniques of the police force," "secret tryst[6] in romantic hotel?" – and then looked for the author: "CK". He hardly dared to raise his head, but then heard Maud asking, "David?" "That bloody woman," he said, and, "I can explain." But where should he begin?

He was almost relieved when his mobile rang and automatically pressed the button that accepted the call. "David?" Alix's voice sounded upset. "I'm at the hospital and have just seen today's *Daily News* … What the hell is this about?" "Alix," David said, trying to think clearly. "It's not what it looks like," he added lamely. "Well, wouldn't you like to explain?" she asked acerbically[7]. "Of course," David said, but again found himself at a loss for

---

1 annotation: Anmerkung  2 to put s.th. down to s.th.: etw. auf etw. zurückführen  3 sports jacket: Sakko  4 to hover: schwanken  5 embrace: Umarmung (liebevoller als der freundschaftliche hug)  6 tryst: Stelldichein  7 acerbic: bissig

words[8]. "It was something else entirely …" Maud, he noticed, was trying to look as if she had no interest whatsoever[9] in listening to what he said, so he started to raise his hand to tell her to leave, but then realised that Rupert Stevenson had entered the room as well. He would demand an explanation!

David desperately thought about what to say to Alix, but all he could come up with was, "I'm so sorry, Alix, I really can't talk right now. I'll get back to you and explain." "Take all the time you need," Alix said angrily, and the next moment she had ended the call. Perplexed, David first looked at the phone's display and then into the faces of Maud and his superior.

"Ouch," Maud said. "We'll leave you to it," Stevenson said and beckoned to Maud to accompany him out of the room. "Come and see me in my office." They closed the door behind them and David speed-dialled[10] Alix's number. All he got was her voicemail.

### Exercise 71

Saying sorry

There are many ways to say that you're sorry. Complete the sentences below by using

*Excuse me – I feel really bad about it – I want to apologise – I was out of order – I'm so sorry – I'm dreadfully sorry – Pardon – Sorry*

Sometimes several answers are possible.

1. (loud voice) Turn the radio down! – _____!

2. (you slightly bump into someone on the bus) – _____.

3. Did I step on your foot? _____!

4. Do you have a moment? _____ for the things I said yesterday. _____ and _____.

5. I forgot our date at the restaurant! _____.

6. _____, may I get through?

7. _____? Did you really say that?

---

8 at a loss for words: sprachlos  9 no … whatsoever: überhaupt kein  10 to speed-dial: eine einprogrammierte Nummer wählen  11 even-tempered: gleichmütig  12 to vent one's anger: seinem Ärger freien Lauf lassen  13 to compromise: beschädigen, aufs Spiel setzen, kompromittieren

"I do not need to tell you that your private life is no concern of mine," Rupert Stevenson, a short time later, pointed out, "but if anything you've done affects your role as SIO, you have to tell me immediately. It's a high-profile case and we cannot run any risks." Stevenson, an even-tempered[11] man, did not vent his anger[12], but David could see that he was seriously provoked. He assured his superior that he had done nothing of the kind and was finally able to – more or less – explain what had happened between him and Nora Palliser. "I was flattered," he concluded, "but it was no more than a friendly hug. There is nothing going on that could compromise[13] my role as SIO."

Then he told Stevenson about his encounter with *Daily News* journalist Cynthia Keefe. "Why didn't you tell me?" Stevenson groaned. "We might have done something to warn them off. And has it occurred to you that this Ms Keefe wanted to get back at[14] you? The photo was probably just what she was waiting for." David said nothing – what was there to say?

"I have to talk to Amal about how to handle this," Stevenson finally said. "I'm not sure how we should react. And you might think about filing an action[15] against the paper. For today, I'd like you to lie low[16] – let Maud do any footwork[17] and concentrate on the things you can do from here. There should be plenty."

David returned to his office and tried to phone Alix, but it was obvious that she had switched off her mobile – which she did but rarely. He left a second message. Alix always got back to him very soon or at least sent a text. He went to see Maud and they spoke about how best to proceed. Afterwards, David tried to call for a third time, to no avail. This wasn't like Alix. In their two-year relationship there had never been silence. They discussed or debated, often even argued about things, and Alix had never refrained from[18] telling him exactly how she felt. But recently, David realised, his own communication had been lacking[19], not only regarding this mess with Nora and the *Daily News*. He had screwed up royally[20].

David went back to Rupert Stevenson's office. "You won't like what I'm going to do now," he said. "Alix isn't answering her phone, so I'll have to go to London." "Today?" Stevenson inquired. "Yes," David answered, "I'm leaving at once." Alix would be home in the early afternoon and he wanted

---

14 to get back at s.o.: (hier) sich an jmd. rächen  15 to file an action against s.o.: jmd. verklagen  16 to lie low: sich unauffällig verhalten  17 footwork: (hier) Arbeit fern vom Schreibtisch  18 to refrain from s.th.: auf etw. verzichten, sich etw. verkneifen  19 to lack: (hier) Mängel aufweisen  20 to screw up royally (ugs.): eine Sache total vermasseln

to be there as soon as possible. "In the midst of this case?" Stevenson asked. "You're absolutely certain?" "Yes, sir."

Stevenson looked at him for what seemed an eternity. "As your superior, I consider this unacceptable," he said coolly and paused. David drew his breath, not being able to figure out how furious his boss really was. "But as a man," Stevenson continued, "I'd find it unacceptable if you did not go."

### Exercise 72

#### Expressing anger

Which expressions can be used in a more formal conversation (1), which are less formal (2) and which is/are a bit vulgar (3)?

*a)* He's a bit peeved. – *b)* He's seething with rage. – *c)* I'm cross with him. – *d)* I'm really mad at him! – *e)* It has made me really angry. – *f)* It's really annoying. – *g)* She is furious about this. – *h)* She's mad as hell at him. – *i)* This is most vexing. – *j)* That really pisses me off!

When Emilia arrived at the agency in the morning, she noticed a very nice car parking in the street – a car she (who openly admitted to a weakness for nice cars) would never be able to afford. But before she could take a closer look, the door of the car opened and Ivor Byrnes got out. "I thought our appointment was for eleven thirty," Emilia was surprised. "There has been … a development," he stated.

They went up the stairs and before they had even taken off their coats Ivor said stiffly, "I have to tell you that the police now consider me a suspect." "Oh," Emilia replied, "do they have any reason to?" If there were strong reasons to suspect Ivor, she thought, surely David would have phoned? "From their point of view, maybe yes," Ivor said. "Would you like to tell me about it?" "It is … sort of private," he stated.

The man was insufferable! "So you're honourably offering to release me from our engagement[21]?" Emilia asked and was pleased to see a small twitch[22] in the corner of Ivor's mouth. "If you want to put it like that, I suppose I am," he replied.

---

21 to honourably release s.o. from an engagement: ehrenvoll nicht darauf bestehen, dass jmd. eine Vereinbarung erfüllt (auch im Sinne des 19. Jhds.: als Ehrenmann nicht auf einer Verlobung bestehen)
22 twitch: Zucken

Emilia sighed. "But what do *you* want?" she asked. "Do you need someone to talk things through with and maybe help with the investigation? Or is the suspicion against you so strong that you should think of consulting a lawyer? In both cases, you'd better be prepared to explain some things you consider private." "I'd like to help with the investigation and clear my name[23] in the process[24]," Ivor said. "I've already phoned my lawyer," he added. "And what did he or she recommend?" "He said that I might think of hiring a private investigator."

Exercise 73

### Phone features

Group the words into threes. Find a description that fits the three words in each group.

*calendar – cell phone – charger[25] – clock – cord – games – headset – landline[26] – receiver – rotary dial[27] – satellite phone – SIM card*

Hours later, Emilia felt that they were going round in circles. Ivor had told her about being blackmailed by Alan Gibson, and the story about his relationship with his dying friend's wife had, in fits and starts[28], come out as well. Emilia saw no reason to condemn Ivor and Beth, who had probably helped each other in this very difficult situation. But what Ivor had told her about the blackmail did not yield[29] much information to go on – he hadn't even kept the photo!

"Alan blackmailed you, so I don't think it unlikely that he blackmailed other people as well," Emilia repeated. She needed to ask David if the police knew anything about it, but would he be forthcoming[30], given who she was working for? "We could of course ask around, if anyone knows about anyone being blackmailed by Alan. But I doubt we'd be successful."

"Let's try another angle," she said some time later. "You said that you gave Alan 20,000 pounds, twice. The sums of money he transferred on the days he noted your initials in the diary were less than 10,000 pounds." Emilia thought. "Has it occurred to you that Alan could have had an

---

23 to clear one's name: seine Unschuld beweisen  24 in the process: dabei  25 charger: Ladegerät
26 landline: Festnetzanschluss  27 rotary dial: Wählscheibe  28 in fits and starts: mit Unterbrechungen, stoßweise  29 to yield: ergeben  30 forthcoming: (hier) mitteilsam

accomplice who he shared the money with?" "He said that he had debts," Ivor remembered, "and I'm sure he also needed to spend some money." "Yes," Emilia said, "but let's not rule[31] the accomplice out. You might not have been the only person Alan blackmailed and the accomplice could have provided him with information." After a pause, she said, "I can't think of anything else right now." "Me neither," Ivor replied gloomily[32].

He sighed. "If only I was rid of Alan Gibson," he said bitterly. "He spied on me, he blackmailed me, he badmouthed[33] me and now his murder makes me a suspect. Sorry. I don't want to give the impression of wallowing in self-pity[34]." No, you probably wouldn't, Emilia thought.

"Wait," she said. "You said that Alan badmouthed you. When was that? And who to?" Observing Ivor's stony face, it was clear that he did not like these questions. He really was an intensely private man, it had been difficult enough for him to tell her what he had told the police. "Did he tell someone about you and Beth?" she asked and a small shift[35] in his face told her that she had hit the mark[36]. But it seemed that she had also hit a raw nerve[37]. "I'll let you do some thinking," she said.

Emilia went into the adjoining[38] room, which she used as her private office. She wanted a few minutes to herself to phone David – she needed to ask him something and maybe he would be able to talk things through with her.

### Exercise 74

**Idioms with "hit"**

There are a number of English idioms with "hit". What do they mean? You might be able to understand them without using a dictionary.

*1. hit a raw nerve – 2. hit a snag – 3. that hit home – 4. hit the bottle – 5. hit rock bottom – 6. hit the roof – 7. hit the hay – 8. hit the mark – 9. hit the road*

David had arrived in London in the early afternoon and gone straight to Alix's flat. Alix didn't answer the bell, so he let himself in with his key and, indecisively, stood in the open plan living room of the ground floor flat. Where was Alix? David hoped that she had only gone out for a short time.

---

31 to rule s.th. out: etw. ausschließen  32 gloomy: niedergeschlagen, pessimistisch  33 to badmouth s.o.: schlecht über jmd. reden  34 to wallow in self-pity: in Selbstmitleid schwelgen  35 shift: Veränderung  36 to hit the mark: ins Schwarze treffen  37 to hit a raw nerve: eine empfindliche Stelle treffen  38 adjoining room: Nebenzimmer

But when he went to the bathroom, he noticed that some toiletries[39] like toothbrush and comb were missing.

He returned to the living room and sat down heavily on the sofa. What should he do now? Could Alix have gone to St Stephen? Could she have gone to see her mother, who lived near St Stephen? Once again, he took out his mobile, to phone Alix for what he felt was the fifteenth time – and to hear her voice on the mailbox.

Then he heard a key turning in the lock[40] of the entrance door – and a male voice asking, "Alix?" For a moment, David found this very strange, but then he recognised the voice as that of Tom Southcote, Alix's landlord and colleague, who lived in the upper storeys[41] of the house. "It's me, David," he said. "Oh thank God," Tom Southcote said. "I thought there was an intruder[42]! I do, of course, much prefer the police." David refrained from remarking that, in other cases, it might have been better to call the police in the first place[43]. "I've come to see Alix," he said, "but it seems that she isn't here."

Tom frowned. "Didn't she tell you?" he asked. "I saw her only for a minute, two hours ago. She said she was going to Devon for the weekend, with a friend. She was, erm, a bit terse[44], as if something … Is everything alright?" "We got our wires crossed[45]," David only said. He didn't want to explain to Tom – who was good-looking, separated from his wife and, David thought, liked Alix a great deal – what had happened and only hoped that Tom had not followed the gossip[46] at the hospital or even seen today's *Daily News!* "Ah," Tom said, with meaning. "Well, I'll leave you alone then."

David sat down again and put his head in his hands. What on earth should he do now? But before he could reach a decision, his mobile began to ring.

"Hi, it's me," Emilia said. "David, do you have a moment?" "I've got all the time in the world," he replied sardonically[47]. "Sorry, Emilia," he added. "Is there anything I can help you with?" "I've got Ivor Byrnes here," she said, "and I'd really like to talk things through with you. There's hardly time now, but Kathy told me that Alan Gibson was an alcoholic and spent time in rehab – could you tell me exactly when?" "I'd have to look it up," he replied, "and I cannot do that right now. But I'll give Maud a call and ask her to get back to you." "Where are you?" Emilia wanted to know. "In

---

39 toiletries: Hygieneartikel  40 lock: Schloss  41 storey: Geschoss  42 intruder: Eindringling, Einbrecher
43 in the first place: von vornherein  44 terse: kurz angebunden  45 to get one's wires crossed: sich missverstehen; auch: schlecht kommunizieren  46 gossip: Klatsch  47 sardonic: sarkastisch

London," he said. "In Alan's flat? Ivor told me that the police …" "No," he cut her short[48], "in Alix's flat. But she's not here."

## Exercise 75

### Interjections

Interjections are frequently used in spoken language. Which of the following

*ah – erm – oh dear – oi – oops – ouch – phew – sigh – yuck – yum*

would you use to express

1. *concern:* _____
2. *delight (seeing delicious food):* _____
3. *disgust:* _____
4. *frustration:* _____
5. *hesitation:* _____
6. *pain (your own or sympathy with another's):* _____
7. *realisation/understanding:* _____
8. *relief:* _____
9. *that you acknowledge a mistake:* _____
10. *that you want to get someone's attention:* _____

"Has anything happened?" Emilia's voice was full of concern and David saw no reason not to tell her. "Have you seen the *Daily News*?" "I saw a copy two days ago, but it's not a paper I usually read." "I'm glad to hear it," he answered dryly, "because of all the ghastly tabloids, it is probably the worst." And he told her what had happened, not even leaving out the infamous[49] headline "Is Darcy's first name David?"

"Oh shit," Emilia finally said, "I'm so sorry." "My thoughts exactly," he replied. "What are you going to do now?" she asked. "I don't know. Return to

---

48 to cut s.o. short: jmd. unterbrechen  49 infamous: (hier) gemein

St Stephen, I think." "I wouldn't do it at once," she said. "What do you mean?" She laughed. "I know it sounds corny[50]," she replied, "but I just thought what would Jane Austen have done? What did she have Mr Darcy do to explain himself?" "How am I supposed to know?" he asked. Emilia sighed. "Write Alix a letter," she said. "Not an email, but a proper[51] letter. Do it right now and then leave it on the table for her to find when she comes back."

David thought. "That might be an idea," he said. "Good," Emilia said. "David, is there anything I can do for you?" she then asked. "No," he said, "unless you can get to the bottom[52] of this darned[53] case before I return." "I'll do my very best," she said. "And, before you begin to write your letter, may I ask a small favour of you?" "Of course," he replied. "Would you," she asked sweetly, "give Maud that call?"

### Exercise 76

### Agreeing

In the two paragraphs above, there are three sentences signalling agreement. Underline them.

In the following list, look for the sentences that completely agree to something (1), that more or less agree with something (2) and that use colloquial or informal language (3).

*a)* That might be an idea. – *b)* You're dead right! – *c)* I agree with your view of the situation. – *d)* I believe that you are right. – *e)* I couldn't agree more. – *f)* You could be right. – *g)* I entirely/wholeheartedly agree with you. – *h)* My thoughts exactly. – *i)* That's probably correct. – *j)* You might have a point. – *k)* You're absolutely right. – *l)* You're bang on!

When Emilia returned to the other room, she heard Ivor say, "I really appreciate this. Thanks a lot – and bye. I hope to see you." He himself had taken the time to make a call and Emilia inquiringly raised an eyebrow.

"I phoned the person we just talked about," he said, rather formally, Emilia thought, "the one Alan told about Beth and me. I remembered something …" "What did you remember?" "Alan told her that he saw Beth and

50 corny: kitschig, schmalzig  51 proper: richtig  52 to get to the bottom of s.th.: einer Sache auf den Grund gehen  53 darned: verflixt

me in a London restaurant, holding hands," he said. "I'm absolutely sure that the photo did not show us in a restaurant, but Alan might have seen us there and decided to spy on us." "Do you remember the restaurants you went to?" she asked. Ivor thought. "I think so, yes, there weren't many. But I do not remember any dates. And anyway – it wouldn't help us if I did."

Emilia was getting annoyed now. "But don't you see?" she asked. "You never know if information might be useful. What you're doing is to carefully select tiny pieces of information that you give to others – but it's difficult for me to work that way! You have to give me room to think, to make sense of things you consider unimportant. You cannot control this investigation like you probably control your life!" She thought that she had probably gone too far, but the words were out and she did not regret them.

### Exercise 77

#### Disagreeing

Consider appropriate responses to the sentences 1 to 4. Take your pick from the following phrases or think of other phrases signalling disagreement.

*The way I see it – In my opinion/From my point of view – If you look at it from another angle – Are you sure? – I think that – You're plain wrong! – I couldn't agree less. – I'm not sure if this is a good idea. – I don't think that*

1. It wouldn't help if I remembered the dates.

2. I'd like to control every step of this investigation.

3. It won't do any good to pursue this line of inquiry.

4. The police are only looking for someone they can charge with the crime.

Ivor looked at her, amazed, and she stared back defiantly[54]. "Beth and I did not often go to restaurants," he then said, and Emilia breathed a sigh of relief, "and when we did, it was in London. It cannot have been more than three or four times, four I believe. Three times we went to an Italian restaurant in Kensington, near Jeremy and Beth's flat. I think it was called

---

54 defiant: herausfordernd, trotzig  55 to reckon: glauben, vermuten

Da Piero. And once we went to a place called Vatel, near my flat. Beth likes French food."

"Could you find out when you went there?" "It must have been in 2010, in spring or early summer," Ivor said. "My diary for that year is in my London flat, I'm afraid. I could call my sister to have a look …" "Do you usually pay by credit card?" Emilia asked, reckoning[55] that Ivor would not have let Beth foot the bill[56]. "Yes, of course!" he replied, "I can even check my credit card activity online, though I don't know if I'll be able to check what I spent two years ago." "Feel free to use my computer," Emilia said, "and let's find out."

David didn't want to waste any more of Alix's writing paper. How hard it was to write what, he agreed with Emilia, was to be a proper letter! He thought that he had got off to a good start, but there were so many things that needed explaining, and many were only becoming clear to him now, by putting them on paper. How had Mr Darcy managed? Did Jane Austen give any pointers? But, not having read *Pride and Prejudice*, he could not avail[57] himself of her advice.

Or could he? He laughed. In a nearby street, where Alix and he often did some shopping, there was a small bookshop cum stationer[58]. He should get some writing paper – and why shouldn't he try to get hold of a copy of *Pride and Prejudice* as well?

The writing paper was easily found, but the book was not. "I'm terribly sorry," the bookseller told David, "we don't have it in stock[59] right now. Do you want me to order it for you?" "No, thanks," David said. "I'm only passing through[60] and just wanted to look something up." The bookseller looked at him. "Do you have a smartphone or something like that?" she asked him. "Yes," David said, remembering that with his tablet computer he could access the wireless network[61] in Alix's flat. "Why?" "You are sure to find the text on the Internet." "The whole book?" David could hardly believe it. "Of course. It was published so long ago that it's in the public domain[62], and you're bound to find a number of e-texts[63] on the Internet."

"That's a great idea," David said, relieved, "thanks a lot." "It's a great book, but not many men seem to want to read it," the bookseller replied drily. "So I help however I can."

---

56 to foot the bill (ugs.): die Rechnung bezahlen  57 to avail oneself of s.th.: von etw. Gebrauch machen, profitieren  58 stationer: Schreibwarengeschäft  59 in stock: vorrätig  60 to pass through: auf der Durchreise sein  61 wireless network: WLAN, drahtloses Netzwerk  62 in the public domain: gemeinfrei (d. h., dass keine Urheberrechte mehr bestehen)  63 e-text (electronic text): digitaler Text (im Internet)

## Exercise 78

Letter writing

Have a look at the salutations[64]

*1. Dear Madam or Sir – 2. Dear Ms Ramsay – 3. Dear Emilia*

and the complimentary closes[65]

*a) All the best – b) Best wishes – c) Kind regards – d) Love –
e) (Best) regards – f) Yours faithfully – g) Yours sincerely*

Which can be used together in a letter?

While Ivor was using the computer, Emilia got a call. "David phoned me," Maud Johnstone explained, "and told me to look up some things for you. I gather you're also working on this case and he told me that you had had a good idea. He didn't explain and seemed to be pressed for time, so, well, I kind of promised that I'd do it. But I'd have to get back to him if you asked anything really sensitive."

Emilia wondered what the idea was David had referred to – but if Maud had promised him, who was she to dissuade her by explaining too much? "I'm really grateful, Maud," she said, "at the moment I only need to know when Alan Gibson was in rehab in 2010." "Oh, that's no problem," Maud replied, "let me see …" She was back soon with the information. "He was in rehab from April 5 to May 14, 2010, and again from September 6 to October 4 the same year, spending the whole time in an alcohol rehab centre near Bournemouth." Emilia thanked her and added that she might be in touch again. "Just call," Maud sighed, "I'll see what I can do."

Emilia and Ivor met, almost triumphantly, when they had both finished their calls. "I had to phone the credit card company," Ivor explained to her, "I can only look up the expenses of the last weeks online. First they said that I could only ask for a hard copy[66] of the credit card statement, but I was able to persuade them to tell me on the phone. I could identify myself with my credit card PIN number, of course." And, of course, the name Ivor Byrnes would have had nothing to do with it, Emilia thought.

64 salutation: (hier) Anrede  65 complimentary close: Schlussformel  66 hard copy: Ausdruck

"They looked for my expenses in 2010," Ivor continued. "I went to Da Piero's on April 29 and May 5, and to Vatel on April 24." "And I've just learned something else," Emilia began, but then she realised that comparing the dates was not going to be of much use. "I'm afraid that Alan was in rehab when you went to those restaurants. He cannot have seen you and Beth."

"Where does that leave us?" Ivor asked Emilia glumly. Both had been silent for a while, trying to make sense of things. "Let's try another point of view," Emilia said. "The possible accomplice – we hadn't ruled him out. So let's say that another person saw you and Beth in the restaurant and passed this information on to Alan, who then blackmailed you. At least it's a theory."

"That is all very well," Ivor replied, "but how are we going to prove this theory? If it is at all possible to prove it …" Yes, how to prove it, Emilia thought – but then she had an idea. Of course! "The beauty of credit cards," she said, "is that most people use them." Ivor gave a wry smile. "It's nice to see you so excited," he said, "but how can we find out who, two years ago, used a credit card in the same restaurants as I did?" "I don't think *we* can," Emilia replied, "but we can try to give the police something to do."

### Exercise 79

Answer the questions

You do not have to write your answers down – practice your spoken English. (See the key to the exercises for suggested answers.)

1. *Why do Emilia and Ivor want to find out about when Ivor went to certain restaurants?*
2. *Why has David gone to London?*
3. *Why is he trying to buy* Pride and Prejudice *in a bookshop?*

Maud Johnstone listened patiently to Emilia's theory, asked a number of questions and then listened some more. "It does sound complicated," she finally said, "but there might be something in it." "So would you do some credit card checks?" "I'm considering[67] it," Maud answered, "but we'd have to check the data of lots of people." Emilia had no idea how much work was involved and how soon the police would set about it, but she ventured[68] to ask, "You couldn't give me a more definitive answer?" "Emilia, I'm doing all I can here," Maud replied huffily[69]. "I'll talk to the colleague who does that kind of check. I need to hear what he says. I'll get back to you."

"We'll have to be content with that," Emilia said to Ivor. "Can nothing else be done?" Ivor asked. "I'm not sure," Emilia replied. "I've thought of finding out from expense accounts[70], but that seems to be even more complicated than getting hold of credit card data." "Yes," Ivor replied. He thought. "But we could try to figure out who worked where at that time. Then we'd have to phone the film studios or theatres ... oh, I don't see how that can be done." "It sounds like another job for the police," Emilia agreed. "I'll have to make another phone call," she said.

Again she went into her private office. She hesitated to phone David now and she hated to suggest that he tell Maud what to do – but it was more than two hours since they had last spoken and he might have finished his letter. If she told him about her theory, maybe he would be easier to convince? She selected his number, only to press the "end" button a moment later. David had switched off his phone. Was this good news or bad news? Emilia asked herself.

She and Ivor spent another two hours thinking about what could be done – which only resulted in Ivor becoming more and more frustrated. Emilia was about to suggest that they call it a day[71], when her phone rang. "I wanted to tell you that we've been making progress," Maud said. "You have to thank Brian Morris for that – and the fact that David doesn't answer his phone." "What kind of progress have you made?" "We've discovered that someone who was at the party also had a meal at the Vatel on April 24, 2010!" "That's splendid!" Emilia exclaimed. "Who is it?" "I'm really not supposed to tell you. We're going to speak to him," Maud said firmly.

Bother[72]! Emilia thought. It was as she had feared – but there might be a way around the reluctance shown by Maud, who, she believed, had not been present when David spoke last to Ivor. Wouldn't the opportunity of meeting Ivor Byrnes entice[73] DS Maud Johnstone?

67 to consider s.th.: über etw. nachdenken  68 to venture: wagen, riskieren  69 huffy: eingeschnappt
70 expense account: Spesenkonto  71 to call it a day: Feierabend machen  72 bother: Mist!  73 to entice: verlocken

"I see," she said. "But Maud, is there anything we can help you with? This theory of ours, it is ... well, I think it's a good idea, but it's only a theory ... so might it not be better to speak to Mr Byrnes before you speak to ... whoever it is? Or to have Mr Byrnes at hand[74]? I mean, he could remember things that might help you."

Maud said nothing, and Emilia hoped that what she had said had made an impact[75]. "You might be right," Maud finally replied. "The problem is," she added, "I need to do this interview at the station and I'm afraid that, since the unfortunate article in today's *Daily News*, we've had some paparazzi here, wanting to get a glimpse of David. I'd really like to avoid a headline which says that Ivor Byrnes is helping the police with their inquiries[76] or is coming to have it out[77] with David or whatever ... But let me see ... Do you think that Mr Byrnes would agree to come to Rosedale Hall in about three quarters of an hour? I'll find him there."

### Exercise 80

Translate

1. Es tut mir so leid, dass ich deinen Geburtstag vergessen habe!

2. Er hat die Sache total vermasselt. Sie ist stocksauer auf ihn.

3. Ich werde mein Bestes tun, diesen verflixten Fall zu lösen.

---

74 to have s.o./s.th. at hand: jmd./etw. in Reichweite haben  75 to make an impact: Wirkung haben
76 to help the police with their inquiries: der Polizei bei ihren Ermittlungen behilflich sein (die Formulierung wird auch verwendet, wenn ein Verdächtiger vernommen wird)  77 to have it out with s.o.: mit jmd. einen Streit austragen

## Chapter 9

"She didn't tell you who they want to question? And you're sure she said 'he'?" Ivor asked, not for the first time. They were on their way to Rosedale Hall, in Ivor's sleek[1] BMW, the mere sight of which had sorely tempted[2] Emilia to ask him to let her do the driving …

"No," she replied. "But she definitely said 'he'. I don't think he's a well-known actor, otherwise she would hesitate to bring him to the police station. He might be a member of the crew, because they're going to Rosedale Hall to fetch him." "Everyone is showing up at Rosedale Hall these days, they're all bored …," Ivor mumbled. "But you went yourself, yesterday," Emilia reminded him. "Did you want to get better acquainted with Pemberley, Mr Darcy? To go through a few scenes with Elizabeth Bennet in your head?" From the driver's seat, Ivor shot her an odd look.

They had almost reached the beginning of the drive to the Hall when a car came out, rather quickly, and turned left. Emilia frowned. This wasn't the way to St Stephen, but from a case that had taken her to Rosedale Hall before she knew that it was not only a film location. Many people worked there.

Ivor accelerated[3] and two minutes later they arrived in the car park near the Hall's visitor entrance, which was well lit by a number of LED lights. There were several cars and, next to one of them, Maud Johnstone was talking intently into a phone, gesticulating with one hand. A police constable was crouching[4] in a bed of low bushes. The young man was looking about rather helplessly, and Emilia suddenly got an uneasy feeling.

Ivor stopped the car abruptly and jumped out, Emilia doing likewise. "We have to block the roads," she heard Maud say, "we cannot let anything happen to the woman."

"What has happened?" Ivor urgently asked the police constable. "Erm, we were on our way to the car with the suspect," the young man stammered, "and there was this woman and he suddenly held a knife to her throat …" "It shouldn't have happened," Maud Johnstone had ended her call. She turned to Emilia. "I'm afraid that Mr Cox panicked and that he managed to flee with a hostage[5]." "Who is this hostage?" Ivor shouted. "It's his colleague,

---

1 sleek: schnittig  2 to sorely tempt: in starke Versuchung führen  3 to accelerate: beschleunigen
4 to crouch: kauern  5 hostage: Geisel

Ms Cochrane," Maud said. "Kathy!" Ivor was looking rather white now, Emilia noticed. "Then why are you not going after him?" he asked. "Before he dragged[6] her into the car, he had me throw the car keys over there," Maud pointed to the bushes, "and we've not managed to retrieve[7] them yet."

### Exercise 81

**Ten words too many**

Cross out the words that should not be in the following text.

*PC Gavin Whitmore tells his girlfriend what happened:*

*"We were going back to the car with the suspect. Kathy Cochrane was there too, because of she had fetched something from her own car. She was looking at us being curiously. We were passing over her car when Christopher Cox jumped forward and I saw that he had been a flick knife[8] in his hand! You know that flick knives are too illegal in the UK? He twisted Kathy's arm and held the knife to her throat. 'You'd better to do what I say,' he snarled and Maud had to throw out our car keys into a thicket! He had Kathy get into the car and, all the while threatening her with the knife, got in himself and drove it off! Maud has had me look for the car keys. It took me many ages to find them and I've scores of pricks in my fingers!"*

"That car. Come on," Ivor said to Emilia, and as quickly as they had got out they got back into the car. "What the heck[9] are you doing?" Emilia heard Maud Johnstone shout, but she only had time for an apologetic shrug before the BMW darted forward[10].

"Did you see what kind of car it was?" Ivor asked between clenched teeth[11], "and do you have any idea where it could be heading?" Emilia had begun to busy herself with the satnav[12]. "I hardly got a glimpse of the car. He might try one of these roads," she said, pointing at the display, "or he might opt for this one, which cuts across the moors and would take him northwards quickly." "You know the area. What do you think?" Ivor asked. "Down here, there are more roads to take," Emilia said slowly, "but they're narrow and go through hamlets. So it would take quite long to really get

---

6 to drag: ziehen, schleifen   7 to retrieve: wiederfinden, zurückholen   8 flick knife: Springmesser   9 what the heck: was zum Kuckuck/Teufel   10 to dart forward: nach vorne schießen   11 clenched teeth: zusammengebissene Zähne   12 satnav (kurz für satellite navigation system): Navi(gationssystem)

away – and if he decides to take one of them, we have no way of knowing which one …" She thought. "Let's take the road across the moors," she decided. "If I remember correctly, you have to stay on it for quite some time, so that would be our chance to catch him."

Ivor sighed. "Alright. We have to hope for the best," he said and put his foot down on the accelerator[13]. Emilia, who herself was what Robert called a spirited driver, hoped that he would slow down a bit when they reached the twisting[14] part of the road that led up the moors. But she was grateful that he seemed to know exactly how to handle the car.

### Exercise 82

**Traffic vocabulary**

Group the words into threes. Find a description that fits the three words in each group.

*stop – car chase – dead slow – no waiting[15] – drive-in cinema – dual carriageway[16] – one way street[17] – give way[18] – no entry – road movie – toll road[19] – no stopping[20]*

There were a number of questions she wanted to ask Ivor, but before she could do so her mobile rang. Knowing who it was she steeled herself[21] for an uncomfortable discussion.

"Emilia?" Maud said matter-of-factly, "I'd rather that you didn't go after Mr Cox, but I'm aware that nothing I say will dissuade you and Mr Byrnes. So don't do anything stupid!" "We won't," Emilia promised. She quickly explained that she thought that Christopher might have taken the road across the moors. "This is our best chance of finding him and Kathy, don't you think?" "I do," Maud replied. "I'm having your mobile phone tracked[22], so keep it switched on! And you'll need a description of the car. It's a grey Saab. I accessed the PNC[23] for the registration number[24]." She gave Emilia the details. "If you see the car, phone me at once and stay in touch. We should try to find out where it is headed and block a road somewhere." "Alright," Emilia said, "but you'd better look for him on the narrow roads near Rosedale too."

---

13 accelerator: (hier) Gaspedal  14 twisting: sich schlängelnd  15 no waiting: Halteverbot  16 dual carriageway: Schnellstraße mit zwei Fahrspuren pro Richtung  17 one way street: Einbahnstraße  18 give way: Vorfahrt achten  19 toll road: mautpflichtige Straße  20 no stopping: Parkverbot  21 to steel oneself: sich wappnen  22 to track a phone: ein Telefon orten  23 PNC: Police National Computer

Then she thought of something. "Did you think of trying to locate Kathy's mobile? In her job, she's constantly on the phone and I believe she always carries it." "Good idea," Maud replied, "but you'd better text me her number." "Will do[25]," Emilia agreed. "I'll be in touch." "Great. And Emilia – I did everything I could to dissuade you!" "Of course you did," Emilia said.

### Exercise 83

Giving advice or stating a preference?

Complete the sentences below by using appropriate forms of "had better" or "would rather" and the verbs in parentheses[26].

1. This morning, David _____ (sleep in), but he thought that he _____ (be late) for work.

2. Maud Johnstone _____ (take along) more than one police constable.

3. Emilia thinks that she _____ (drive) the car! She _____ (be sick) on the passenger seat.

The car sped around a hairpin bend[27] – making Emilia queasy[28] – and reached a straight stretch of road. This gave her the chance to send her text message and to open the road atlas she had discovered in the glove compartment[29] of the car. Then the road climbed again, but Ivor drove a bit more slowly. "We cannot take any risks," he explained, "I couldn't care less about Christopher, but I won't let anything happen to Kathy."

"There is something you're not telling me," Emilia said. "It's not the first time you've criticised me for that," he replied. "Not exactly for that," Emilia said. She thought and decided to risk the question. "Why do I get the distinct[30] impression that I'm suddenly part of a Jane Austen plot?"

Ivor sighed. "Come on," Emilia said. "For weeks, all you and Kathy do is bicker, and now you're desperate to help her. And when I last met Kathy …" She laughed. Suddenly it all fell into place[31]!

"What was I to do?" Ivor asked, throwing her a helpless look so comic that she had to suppress another laugh. "Put yourself in my shoes. What is

---

24 registration number: Autonummer  25 will do (ugs.): wird gemacht  26 parentheses: runde Klammern  27 hairpin bend: Spitzkehre  28 to make s.o. queasy: dazu führen, dass jmd. übel wird  29 glove compartment: Handschuhfach  30 distinct: eindeutig  31 to fall into place: Sinn ergeben (so wie sich die Teile eines Puzzlespiels zu einem Bild zusammenfügen)

a man to do, who, playing the hero in the screen adaptation of everyone's favourite novel, suddenly discovers that his own life is becoming embarrassingly[32] like this novel? And who is constantly pursued by the media?" He paused. "I'm sorry for hiding from you that it was Kathy who Alan told about my relationship with Beth." "She didn't tell me either," Emilia replied. "But she said something about her misjudging people and was rather cut up[33] about it. So you clashed[34] about what Alan told her. What did you do then? Let me guess …" "I wrote her a letter," Ivor said dryly.

### Exercise 84

Phrases to do with films

Find the German equivalents for the English phrases and idioms.

*1. film for the big screen – 2. film for the small screen – 3. to capture on film – 4. to catch a film – 5. to screen a film – 6. to share the screen – 7. to turn s.th. into a film*

*a) etw. verfilmen – b) einen Film vorführen – c) etw. im Film festhalten – d) Fernsehfilm – e) gemeinsam auf der Leinwand zu sehen sein – f) Kinofilm – g) sich einen Film ansehen*

David had caught the 19:29 from Liverpool Street Station just in time. He was exhausted. It had taken him some time to finish his letter to Alix. He had looked up Darcy's letter to Elizabeth in the e-book of *Pride and Prejudice* and had even scanned the chapters leading up to it: The protagonist had singularly[35] failed to communicate and here the novel bore an uncomfortable resemblance to his own situation! The first part of Darcy's letter sounded very bitter and even offensive, but then the tone had changed and the writer had suddenly appeared much more likeable. He had revealed his most private thoughts and feelings and it had cost him. Jane Austen's letter did not wholly apply[36] to his own case, David felt – he refused to think of himself as a rejected[37] lover! and his letter to Alix needed to be much more personal –, but it had given him some much-needed distance and a fresh perspective about how to proceed. Now all he could do was to

---

32 embarrassing: peinlich  33 cut up: niedergeschlagen, erschüttert  34 to clash: aneinandergeraten
35 singular: einzigartig, außerordentlich  36 to apply to s.th.: (hier) sich auf etw. beziehen (lassen)
37 rejected: zurückgewiesen, verschmäht

hope that his letter would have a similar effect as the fictional one seemed to have had.

David leaned back in his seat. All he wanted to do was sleep, but it wasn't only his private life that needed sorting out … He sat up straight. He had turned off his mobile, hours ago, and then completely forgotten about it. Damn, he thought, took the phone from the pocket of his coat and switched it on: He had missed twelve calls altogether, five from Maud Johnstone alone, three from an unknown number and a number of texts, among them one from Nora Palliser: "So very sorry C U l8er? Nora". He didn't bother to listen to his messages or to answer them, instead he pressed the button to return Maud's last call.

Exercise 85

### Text messages

Because they have to be short, text messages have developed their own language (also called textese) full of abbreviations. Some of them are also frequently used in emails.

Do you know what the following text abbreviations mean?

*1. b/c – 2. B4 – 3. C U l8er – 4. GR8 – 5. HAND –*
*6. IMO – 7. LOL – 8. THNX – 9. 2day*

"It started with the first meetings for the series," Ivor said, not taking his eyes off the road. "I liked Kathy at once. In the beginning I fought the attraction. I thought that it wouldn't be professional, might put her in an uncomfortable situation, and that I'd better wait until after the filming. But that didn't work. I'm afraid that I behaved rather stiffly towards her, and she reacted by giving me witty[38] answers. You know that she's always quick with a repartee[39]. I hoped that she liked me and I liked her more and more."

"When Nicholas threw[40] that party at our house, which everyone calls Netherfield, I did not want to deny myself the pleasure of dancing with her. I allowed myself to hope, but an hour later she had simply disappeared. And then everything suddenly changed with Alan's murder. The morning after the press event I saw Kathy storming out of the room where the police

---

38 witty: frech und geistreich  39 quick with a repartee: schlagfertig  40 to throw a party (ugs.): eine Party schmeißen

were doing their interviews and she was really upset. I knocked on her door and when she opened it I realised that she was crying. It was obvious that she was not expecting me. I tried …," here Ivor was stumbling a bit, "I offered her a shoulder to cry on and tried to show her how I felt, but she wouldn't have any of it and said something like I was making a habit[41] of consoling distraught women. I could imagine what she was alluding to and then she suddenly threw what Alan had told her at me! I did not know what …," Ivor stopped abruptly. "There's a car!" he exclaimed.

### Exercise 86

**Answer the questions**

1. Why do Emilia and Ivor follow Christopher Cox's car?

2. What does Maud Johnstone have to say about this?


They were on the moors now, on a vast expanse of what Emilia knew was bog[42] and withered[43] heather, eerily[44] illuminated by the pale light of the moon. And there, quite far away, they could make out the lights of a car that seemed not to be moving. "Let's hope it's him," she said. "But it's too early to say, we have to get nearer." "Yes," Ivor agreed.

"What do we do if it's him?" Emilia asked. Ivor was silent. "I don't know," he finally said. "I'd love to have it out with him, but he has a knife and it would be silly to risk him doing something to Kathy …" He drove steadily on, but they had not got much nearer when they saw that the car was moving again. "It could be him," Emilia said. She had been busy with the satnav again and had had a look at the road atlas on her lap. "There are only a few paths around here, so it's not so very likely that it's someone else."

She took her mobile and quickly selected Maud's number. "We may have seen him," she said, excited, "do you know where we are?" "We've only just managed to set everything up at the station," Maud said, "but we're picking up signals from your mobile and from Kathy's, I'm glad to say. It seems that you're in the same cell[45]. The cells are quite large where you are, so we cannot locate you exactly, but you seem not to be too far away from each other." "Kathy's mobile signal is coming from somewhere

---

41 to make a habit of s.th.: sich etw. zur Gewohnheit werden lassen  42 bog: Sumpf  43 withered: welk, verblüht  44 eerie: unheimlich, gespenstisch  45 cell: Zelle (hier eines Mobilfunknetzes)

near us, so it has to be his car," Emilia quickly said to Ivor, who gave a sigh of relief. "Do you have any idea where on the moors you are?" she heard Maud asking. "It's hard to say," Emilia was looking at the road atlas again, "but I think that we're about five miles away from a turnoff[46], but it's a kind of track that doesn't go anywhere, it only returns to the road we're on, so there's a second turnoff after a mile … then there's a couple of miles to a road crossing, and," she had another look, "from there he could go east or west or north, where he'd meet the A 171. There are bound to be more cars there, which he's probably hoping for."

"Alright," Maud said. "It will take you some time to get there, so we'll see what we can do. By the way, David phoned." "So he hasn't disappeared," Emilia said, "where is he?" "On the train," Maud said. "When I told him, he cursed like a sailor. I won't repeat what he said, but he begs[47] you to be careful."

### Exercise 87

**Types of roads**

Complete the sentences using the terms

*A road – B road – bypass – congestion – crossroads – junction (2x) – motorway – roundabout – straight on – turn left – turn right*

1. *An intersection of roads is called* _____ *or* _____. *The last term is also used where a road leads to a motorway. A circular intersection of roads is referred to as* _____.

2. *Many main roads in Britain are* _____. _____ *are local roads. Both are numbered, as are* _____, *which are designed for high-speed traffic and are only accessible at a number of* _____.

3. *A* _____ *avoids a town or village to reduce noise and* _____ *there.*

4. *If you continue on one and the same road, you drive* _____. *To change roads you* _____ *or* _____.

---

46 turnoff: Abzweigung  47 to beg s.o.: jmd. inständig bitten

"And it was then that you wrote the letter?" Emilia, having ended the call, asked Ivor. "Do you need to know everything?" he groaned. "I merely want to hear the rough outline of the story we're in," she replied sweetly, "and I am well aware that you'll sue[48] me if anything gets out."

"Yes, that was when I wrote the letter," he said. "It wasn't a handwritten one, it would have been illegible[49]. I wrote it on my computer, printed it out and slipped it under Kathy's door. And then I came to see you. I didn't mistrust the police, I think Inspector Rowe is a decent enough chap, even if I wonder what is going on with him and Nora. But I simply had to do something."

"The next day I got a text from Kathy, saying that she was dreadfully sorry and that she hoped to see me soon to apologise in person. She does not, of course, have to apologise for anything, but I took the text as an encouragement[50]. So I went to Rosedale Hall, where I knew she was. We talked, until Inspector Rowe interrupted us. And that is the 'rough outline' of the story. You know the rest."

"Thank you for telling me," Emilia simply said. It was a lovely story and she dearly hoped for a happy ending.

Soon after, they passed the turnoffs Emilia had described to Maud and left the high moors. The road, with many bends, began to descend and then the wide landscape spread before them in the moonlight, with the road winding down and a few house lights in the distance. What, however, they couldn't see were the lights of a car.

"Damn," Ivor cursed and stopped the car abruptly. "We've lost him." "Wait a few seconds," Emilia said, "the car could reappear from behind a hill or dry stone wall. We cannot see very well." They waited. But there was no car. "Where did we lose him?" Ivor asked. "He cannot have switched off the car lights!" He was really alarmed now. "I hope not," Emilia replied. "It would be madness."

"Turn the car around," she said a moment later. Ivor gave her an inquiring look, but only saw her consulting the road atlas again and did as he was bid. "There were two turnoffs, but they belong to a very narrow road that leaves and rejoins[51] this one," Emilia explained. "I didn't think that he'd take it, but he may have noticed a car behind him and decided not to take any risks. He may have waited there for us to overtake him or even taken the road back!"

---

48 to sue s.o.: jmd. verklagen  49 illegible: unleserlich  50 encouragement: Ermutigung  51 to rejoin s.th.: (hier) wieder zu etw. zurückkehren

## Exercise 88

### Find the (relative) opposites

*arthouse film – black and white film – box-office hit – colour film – flop – B movie – lead – postproduction – romcom – silent film – preproduction – splatter film – talkie – walk-on part*

---

Ivor raced the car back to the nearest turnoff and then stopped. "Let me out here," Emilia said and opened the door. "You follow this small road," she showed him on the map. "If you find the car, drive on, give the police a call and pick me up. You must drive on, don't confront him! If you don't find him, he'll either be passing here, where I'll at least see him, or he'll be going back. I'll alert[52] the police to this possibility. "Are you sure you want to stay here – all alone?" Ivor asked. She nodded. "If I crouch down there," she pointed to a place near the road hidden in the shadows, "he won't be able to see me."

Emilia got out of the car, Ivor drove off and she crouched down where she had said she would. It was cold and windy on the vast and windswept[53] surface of the moors, which was lent a sinister[54] aspect by the eerie light of the moon. She got out her mobile and called Maud, quickly explaining what they had decided to do. "The police are on their way to the crossing you described," Maud said, "and I'll be sending two cars the way you came. I only hope that they'll be in time."

After the call there was nothing to do but wait. In her crouching position, Emilia was cold and uncomfortable and she tried to keep her mind off all the things that could happen. Sometimes she looked at the watch on the display of her mobile. Ten minutes since she saw Ivor, fifteen, twenty. The three-quarter circle the narrow road described had seemed to be to her no more than six miles, seven at the most, but she couldn't say what kind of road it was and how long it would take to drive it. She waited for what seemed to be a very long time.

Then she first saw the lights of a car and then heard it approaching quickly. She stayed in her crouched position and watched it coming nearer. But suddenly, at quite some distance from her, the car stopped and Emilia

---

52 to alert: alarmieren, aufmerksam machen  53 windswept: windgepeitscht  54 sinister: unheimlich, unheilvoll

could just see that somebody got out. Was it Ivor getting out of his car? Emilia jumped up to get a better view. In the moonlight she could make out that the person – a man, she thought – was probably opening one of the car's back doors. He wrenched[55] out something which Emilia believed was a second person, whom he left in the middle of the road! Was it Kathy? What had Christopher done to her? Emilia had to restrain[56] herself to remain where she was. She crouched down again and waited until the man got back into the car, drove on and – finally! – passed the place where she was hiding.

### Exercise 89

#### Translate

1. *Emilia war sehr versucht, David anzurufen und ihn zu fragen, ob er seinen Brief fertig geschrieben hatte.*

2. *Jessica hofft, dass Nicholas das Veranstalten von Partys nicht zur Gewohnheit werden lässt.*

3. *Emilia muss sich zurückhalten, Ivor nicht zu viele persönliche Fragen zu stellen.*


Emilia jumped up and ran to where the person was lying. It was indeed Kathy, lying with her back to Emilia, and she did not move! The first thing to do, however, was to get her off the street, which Emilia did as soon as she had reached the spot.

Kathy gave a moan. "It's me, Emilia," Emilia said, "are you OK?" She gently touched the other woman and, on her wrists, felt what appeared to be some kind of tape[57]. "What are *you* doing here?" Kathy asked faintly. "Looking for you, of course," Emilia replied. Then she saw the lights of another car approaching. "And here's Ivor. Let's ask him to give us a lift."

Not long before Emilia had had to be satisfied with Ivor telling her the rough outline of his story, and she had not wanted to pry. But she took no inconsiderable[58] pleasure in witnessing what was happening now – miles away from all the places the paparazzi had thought to station themselves:

---

55 to wrench out: herauszerren  56 to restrain oneself: sich zurückhalten  57 tape: (hier) Klebeband
58 not inconsiderable: nicht unbeträchtlich

Ivor Byrnes, the famous actor, jumped out of the car, raced towards where Kathy and Emilia were and gathered Kathy in his arms. And if Emilia had harboured any doubts[59] about Kathy returning his feelings, she soon knew better.

She had, however, before long witnessed enough of this intensely private happy ending, got up and, in the car, looked for the first-aid kit[60]. There she found scissors to cut the leucoplast tape Christopher had bound Kathy's hands and feet with. She handed the scissors to Ivor and then sat in the driver's seat and waited. She was pretty sure that Ivor would agree to let her drive his car back.

### Exercise 90

Talking about newspapers

Form sentences containing the words "broadsheet(s)" and "tabloid(s)" and the following keywords. Suggestions can be found in the key to the exercises.

1. *newspaper formats, types of newspapers*
2. *paparazzi, serious or investigative journalism*
3. *glaring headlines, personal lives of celebrities, smaller headlines, more information*
4. *sensational stories, gossip columns, politics, culture, economy*
5. *photos of scantily clad[61] women, photos of men in business suits*

---

59 to harbour doubts: Zweifel hegen  60 first-aid kit: Verbandskasten  61 scantily clad: leicht bekleidet

# Chapter 10

David was not altogether[1] surprised that, when he arrived at the police station later in the evening, everything was in uproar[2]. Outside, journalists had stationed themselves. David had been warned by Maud Johnstone that they had got wind that something had happened. He had to make his way through them and fend off questions he could hardly answer, having only been informed of the essential facts. When he finally entered the police station, he was greeted by the desk sergeant, who triumphantly said, "We've got him!"

He found Maud in the incident room[3], together with several police officers, Emilia, Ivor Byrnes and Kathleen Cochrane. All were talking excitedly. "I've only been away for a few hours and you've solved the case," he said to make himself noticed.

"So you're back," Emilia greeted him. "I thought I might be needed here, but it appears that I was mistaken," David replied and then smiled. "Congratulations to you all," he said. "How exactly did you get him?"

Near the A 171 the road from the moors branched out in many directions, but the police, Maud explained, had been able to block a number of roads there. And at one of these road blocks Christopher Cox's attempt to escape had ended. "We were lucky that he decided to cross the moors," she said. "If he had opted[4] for one of the narrow roads near Rosedale, there wouldn't have been time to react like we did and our task would have been much more difficult." "He was upset when he realised that he had to stay on the same road for miles and miles," Kathy remarked dryly. "He should have had a closer look at the satnav in his car, but before he stopped and tied my hands and feet he was much too busy to do so. It's kind of inconvenient if you have to drive and, at the same time, hold a knife to someone."

"Have you spoken to him?" David asked Maud, who was suddenly looking like the cat that got the cream[5]. "He's waiting for us," she said.

---

1 altogether: (hier) wirklich, gänzlich  2 uproar: Tumult, Erregung  3 incident room: Einsatzzentrale (der einem wichtigen Kriminalfall gewidmete Raum)  4 to opt for s.th.: sich für etw. entscheiden  5 to look like the cat that got the cream: sehr selbstzufrieden aussehen

## Exercise 91

## Animal idioms

Match the English idioms, which include animals, and their German counterparts.

*1. the early bird catches the worm – 2. everyone and his dog – 3. monkey business – 4. to avoid the elephant in the room – 5. to put lipstick on a pig – 6. to put the cart before the horse – 7. to trust the cat to keep the cream*

*a) das (auffällige) Problem ignorieren – b) den Bock zum Gärtner machen – c) etw. schönreden – d) etw. falsch herum anfangen – e) Gott und die Welt – f) eine krumme Tour – g) Morgenstund hat Gold im Mund*

But as it turned out, the case was far from solved. It was obvious that Christopher Cox's actions were those of a guilty man – but the suspect refused to say a word. He insisted on a lawyer he knew, who had to come up from London and only arrived late on Saturday morning. And even in a first interview with his lawyer present Christopher said hardly anything.

It was only on Saturday evening, after several private discussions with his lawyer, that Christopher Cox finally decided to make a full confession[6] – although "confession" was not the word he used and David could not help but feel that he had carefully constructed a narrative[7] that would show him in the best light.

"I've made a number of mistakes and it took me some time to realise that I've been making things worse," Christopher began, in a contrite[8] voice. What followed was his version of events: Five years before, he and Alan Gibson had begun to look for "other sources[9] of income, to make ends meet[10]". At that time, Alan earned almost nothing and Christopher's jobs were hardly profitable. It was only later that he began to be hired as an assistant director and earned more money more regularly. "We felt that we were treated unfairly," he explained, "and we simply had to find a way to make a living."

One evening, "after getting drunk in Alan's squalid[11] bedsit[12] in Tottenham," Christopher had told Alan a scandalous piece of gossip he had

---

6 confession: Geständnis  7 narrative: Erzählung; auch: Argumentation  8 contrite: reumütig  9 source: Quelle  10 to make ends meet: über die Runden kommen  11 squalid: armselig, dreckig  12 bedsit: (möbliertes) Zimmer ohne eigenes Bad

got wise[13] to and they had toyed with the idea of getting money out of this information. A few days later, Christopher claimed, Alan had phoned him and suggested that they act[14] on this idea. For him, things were getting desperate and he proposed to do the actual blackmailing, if Christopher would provide him with information. Christopher had, after some hesitation and with a number of misgivings[15], agreed, and so they had begun a profitable business.

"We did not take money from anyone who couldn't afford it," Christopher sought[16] to vindicate[17] himself. "And it made all the difference to us. Alan was able to seek medical help for his drink problem and to rent a better flat. He first moved to a larger bedsit in Bloomsbury and then to a rather nice flat in Hampstead. This gave him hope. Do not underestimate[18] what a squalid Tottenham bedsit can do to you."

Christopher was surprisingly forthcoming about the people he and Alan had blackmailed. The reason for this was, as David later learned, that he somehow suspected that Alan had made a number of notes about the money he had extorted[19] and had thought it wise not to deny something that would come to light anyway.

"The night of the party," Christopher Cox explained, "Alan told me, out of the blue[20] and in no uncertain terms, that he wanted to end our business arrangement. He had been cast in a good role and more would follow, so I could understand why he wanted to end it, but I thought that he should have had the decency[21] to wait until the moment was good for both of us. I have recently bought a flat and this job is, was …, one of the first jobs that paid really well. I told him that I needed to be more financially secure before I could think about doing without the extra money."

"Alan, however, did not see things the same way. He wanted to end it at once, which put me in a precarious position. We quarrelled, not as loud as Kathy and Alan did later, and Alan threatened to go to James Riddell and tell him all about it. I'm not sure he would have delivered on that threat[22] – it would have been a case of the pot calling the kettle black[23] – but he might have done and might have found a way of seriously misrepresenting the role I played. I could not take that risk and decided that we had to talk some more."

---

13 to get wise to s.th.: etw. spitzkriegen  14 to act on s.th.: entsprechend etw. handeln  15 misgivings: Bedenken  16 to seek: (hier) sich bemühen  17 to vindicate oneself: sich rechtfertigen  18 to underestimate: unterschätzen  19 to extort money: Geld abnötigen  20 out of the blue: aus heiterem Himmel, urplötzlich  21 to have the decency: den Anstand besitzen  22 to deliver on a threat: eine Drohung wahrmachen

### Exercise 92

Idioms with colours

Find the two idioms that include colours in the paragraphs above and German translations for the following:

*1. as white as a sheet – 2. to talk until one is blue in the face – 3. green with envy – 4. to be tickled pink – 5. to have plenty of grey matter*

The way Christopher Cox had lured[24] Alan Gibson – and his car – into the lay-by and what had happened next did not become wholly clear to David. The way Christopher represented it, he and Alan had agreed to meet there. But to David a windy lay-by in the middle of the Yorkshire moors in a cold November night seemed a particularly uncomfortable place to meet – especially when one considered the fact that the men had been on their way to the hotel they were both staying at. In his opinion, Christopher had left the party early and waited in his car for Alan Gibson to leave as well. It was likely that he preceded[25] Alan in his car and somehow blocked the narrow road between Moreton and St Stephen. Alan might have got out of his car then and asked what was the matter and the two men might have continued their discussion in the lay-by.

There, Christopher claimed, Alan had become violent. They had fought and Alan had slipped, regrettably hitting the back of his head on one of the stones placed where the lay-by abutted[26] the steep decline into the valley below. This was another matter David had serious doubts about – the SOCOs[27] had thoroughly examined the lay-by and would have found traces on the stone, the position of which Christopher couldn't describe convincingly. David strongly suspected that he had taken a tool or sports bat[28] from the boot[29] of his car – or had picked up one of the smaller stones lying about – and had hit Alan with it. Whether he had really done so, and whether it had been done with the intent to kill[30], remained to be determined[31] in court: Despite the persistent questioning of the police, Christopher Cox stuck to his version of events – that Alan had slipped unluckily.

In David's opinion this was also contradicted by Christopher's decision to fake the car accident, which the accused[32] explained as a panic reaction.

23 the pot calling the kettle black: (etwa) jmd. etw. vorwerfen, dessen man selbst schuldig ist  24 to lure: locken  25 to precede: vorangehen, -fahren  26 to abut s.th.: an etw. grenzen  27 SOCOs: Scene of Crime Officers  28 sports bat: für einen Sport verwendeter Schläger  29 boot: Kofferraum  30 intent to kill: Tötungsvorsatz  31 to determine: (hier) herausfinden, feststellen  32 accused: Beschuldigter

"I simply panicked," he said. "I thought that if I called the police or left him lying there to be found there would be an inquest. I was afraid that nobody would believe that his death was an accident. Now I see that what I did was utterly[33] wrong, but I was in quite a state[34]. I thought, or rather hoped, that, in a rural area like this, things would be more … laid-back[35], that everyone would say that Alan must have veered[36] off the road and driven his car into the abyss[37], and that an autopsy would not be considered necessary. I hoped that the injuries incurred in the car crash would make everyone believe that he died in a car accident." This, David thought, was not very complimentary[38] to the Yorkshire police, but he knew that without the witness the "accident" would probably not have got immediate attention and the examination of the body might not have been as thorough.

### Exercise 93

Missing words

Ten words are missing from the following text. Can you find out which words?

*It a piece of luck that Gregory Lever heard a crash that night. But police should also be grateful to Daisy – do remember the elderly dog had to be taken out for a leak? Well, Daisy thinks that her master become much more patient with her. She is also very pleased all the doggie treats[39] given to her the neighbours. And after reading in the local paper an arrest had made, Gregory whispered her that they had certainly done their bit to help catch a murderer!*

"But we launched a murder investigation," David reminded him. "Why didn't you come forward then to explain things?" "I was afraid that you wouldn't believe me," Christopher Cox justified himself. You said it! David thought. The man had no idea that he was getting himself into hot water[40].

"I decided to hope for the best," Christopher continued. "But the last few days have been terrible. When you came to Rosedale on Thursday looking for Ivor, and then spoke to him for a long time, I began to be afraid that you were on to the blackmail. The police have probably been investigating everyone's financial affairs, I thought, and have been searching

---

[33] utterly: ganz und gar  [34] to be in a state: in großer Unruhe, verzweifelt sein  [35] laid-back: entspannt
[36] to veer off the road: von der Straße abkommen  [37] abyss: Abgrund  [38] complimentary: (hier) schmeichelhaft  [39] doggie treat: Hundeleckerei  [40] in hot water (ugs.): in schwerer Verlegenheit

Alan's flat – and I really couldn't say if Alan had not written down anything about our … business."

"But going to London to search Alan's flat was out of the question. With all the CCTV cameras around, there wouldn't have been a snowflake's chance in hell[41] that I wouldn't be noticed somewhere. Besides, I suspected that the police would have got to the flat earlier than I could have. So I decided to wait. There might be damning[42] evidence in Alan's flat – or there might be nothing on me. I thought about leaving the country at once, but I rather fancied[43] my job as AD … so I decided to stay put[44] and sit it out. But I did prepare myself for the eventuality[45] of having to get away. An aunt of mine has a cottage in Northumberland, and I thought I might lie low there and then try to get abroad somehow."

"When the police came looking for me I knew that the game was up[46]. Your Sergeant and the Constable were walking beside me, but – fortunately, I then thought – there was Kathy in the car park, and the day before I had equipped[47] myself with a knife. I did not mean (1) to do her any harm, but taking her was my only chance to get away (2). I planned (3) to set her free as soon as possible, but then I noticed a car that could have been following (4) me and it was rather difficult to get rid of her. But I did not want her to suffer … and I didn't want another person to die! Alan's death is an accident I'll regret for the rest of my life."

Exercise 94

## Choose the right word

In the paragraph above, there are verbs marked 1 to 4. Which of the following verbs could replace them?

1. *aim – contemplate – propose – intend*
2. *get on – get along – escape – break out*
3. *intended – arranged – scheduled – contrived*
4. *succeeding – pursuing – haunting – persecuting*

---

41 not a snowflake's chance in hell (ugs.): überhaupt keine Chance  42 damning: vernichtend  43 to fancy s.th. (ugs.): etw. sehr gerne mögen  44 to stay put: sich nicht vom Fleck rühren  45 eventuality: Möglichkeit  46 the game is up (ugs.): das Spiel ist aus  47 to equip oneself with s.th : sich mit etw. ausrüsten

Kathleen Cochrane's testimony[48] – which the police had been able to take some time before Christopher Cox deigned[49] to say a word – completed the statement of the accused. She had noticed Ivor Byrnes and Alan Gibson acting decidedly cool towards each other. In one of her conversations with Alan she had commented on this and, after a number of evasive[50] replies, which Kathy had refused to believe, Alan had finally told her that their relationship had deteriorated[51] when he had learned of Ivor's relationship with Beth Froy. "I happened to see them together in a restaurant in London," Alan had told Kathy, "and from the way they were holding hands and looking at each other it was clear that there was something going on between them at the time when Jeremy was dying. I thought this very strange."

As a result of this chance encounter[52], Alan had explained, he had been anxious to put some distance between himself and Ivor, while Ivor had treated him with cold disdain[53]. "When James cast Ivor as William Darcy and Alan as Andrew Fitzwilliam," Kathy said, "both were not pleased to have to work together and it showed. Alan asked me not to tell anyone about Ivor and Beth – as if I'd have! It was, after all, their private affair –, but he thought that Ivor might have taken advantage of Beth's situation. I'm afraid that I believed him."

She also explained that during his flight Christopher had realised that someone was following him. With Kathy incapacitated[54] by the surgical tape from the car's first-aid kit, he had had a closer look at the satnav and decided to circle back along the small side road[55], hoping to give the other car the slip by letting it overtake him. "But Ivor followed him, and shortly before returning to the main road Christopher saw the lights of his car," she explained. "When he suddenly stopped I had no idea why, but then I realised that he wanted to be rid of me. He said that he was certain that whoever was following would pick me up and end his pursuit." She stopped, and then continued in a much lower voice. "He dragged me out of the car and left me in the middle of the road. That was when I really began to be afraid. I could only hope that the other car would not see me too late …" Which would have been another way for Christopher Cox to stop his pursuer, David grimly thought.

---

48 testimony: Zeugenaussage  49 to deign to do s.th.: sich zu etw. herablassen  50 evasive: ausweichend
51 to deteriorate: sich verschlechtern  52 chance encounter: zufällige Begegnung  53 disdain: Verachtung
54 to incapacitate: außer Gefecht setzen  55 side road: Nebenstraße

### Exercise 95

In the know – or not?

In the paragraph above, underline the expression which means that someone knows something and the one which means that someone doesn't. Which of the following sentences signal that you know something and which signal that you do not?

*1. Beats me. – 2. I don't have a clue. – 3. I don't know the first thing about it. – 4. I have a very good idea that … – 5. I have it from the horse's mouth. – 6. I'm all at sea. – 7. I'm out of my depth here. – 8. I'm positive that … – 9. I'm very much aware of this. – 10. I've been brought up to date. – 11. I'm safe in the knowledge … – 12. Your guess is as good as mine.*

---

Emilia, in the aftermath[56] of the dramatic events on the moors, was trying to complete her own picture of what had happened. She knew that David was busy getting a confession out of Christopher Cox and that she would learn about it in time[57]. But what *she* wanted to find out was something she did not think the police would be interested in. So she was happy that Kathy agreed to visit her at home on Sunday.

Kathy brought a rather magnificent bunch of flowers and a bottle of wine. "Ivor sends his very best regards," she said. "He has told me all about what happened, that it was you who put the police on the right track[58], and I'd like to thank you properly. We both would." "That is very kind," Emilia replied, "but it was you who had to suffer. It must have been quite an ordeal[59]." "It was," Kathy admitted, "but I cannot say that it was a bad thing. It ended so very happily."

Emilia smiled. "I have to admit that I was a bit surprised about that," she said. "It was quick, wasn't it? When did you start to like Ivor?" "I do not know exactly when it began," Kathy replied and hesitated. "I believe it must have been when I first saw the beautiful car he jumped out of," she said, her eyes sparkling. Emilia had to laugh. "Do be serious!" she said.

"It was a bit more complicated than that," Kathy conceded. "I had noticed that Ivor was looking at me a great deal. And I realised that many things he said and did were really bothering[60] me. But it took me some time

---

56 aftermath: Folge  57 in time: (hier) schließlich, zum rechten Zeitpunkt  58 track: (hier) Spur  59 ordeal: Qual, Tortur  60 to bother s.o.: jmd. etw. ausmachen

to work out that what he thought also mattered a lot to me." Emilia nodded. "I see," she said.

"At that time," Kathy continued, "I believed that he was interested in Nora. They seemed to be getting along so well, and it did not help that they did all this subtle[61] flirting when they were acting their scenes, while I had to order everyone around. And with me, Ivor was acting so very properly[62]! I couldn't make him out and my own reactions to him were quite contradictory. Then Alan told me about Ivor's relationship with Beth and that he was sure that Ivor had taken advantage of Beth's situation and I … I think that I was glad to have found a reason not to like him."

### Exercise 96

#### Sending one's regards

In the paragraphs above, you might have noticed an expression for "Grüße ausrichten". Combine the words in the left and in the right column to form sentences sending regards. Sometimes there are several options.

1. *Give my love*              a) *to Inspector Rowe.*
2. *Give my regards*           b) *to say hello.*
3. *Mr Rutherford sends*       c) *to your father.*
4. *Charles asked me*          d) *to Mum.*
5. *Remember me*               e) *his best wishes.*

"After Alan had been killed and the police had not believed what I said I had done after the party, I really couldn't take any more[63]. That was when Ivor came to my room at the hotel and … well, I'm afraid that we managed to have a terrible row. And shortly afterwards, I got his letter. It was a really good letter, Ivor can be very eloquent if he chooses. Then we began to talk and to sort out the things we had misunderstood about each other. But what happened on Friday evening certainly sped up things between us! It was so lucky that you were there when Chris threw me out of his car. And that Ivor was there as well was … quite unbelievable."

---

61 subtle: (hier) unterschwellig  62 proper: (hier) korrekt  63 not to be able to take any more: mit den Kräften am Ende sein

They smiled at each other. "Now I understand," Emilia said contentedly. After a pause, she added, "There is one last question I have. Did *you* tell Ivor that I'm a private investigator?" "I didn't," Kathy said, "but he confessed that he sometimes listened[64] to us talking and laughing in the kitchen – he was quite embarrassed to admit to it. It was then that he overheard[65] you telling me what you did professionally. And after our quarrel he thought that he needed to do something to help clear up the mess we were all in. So he hired you." "Maybe he also thought that hiring me might earn him a few brownie points[66] with you?" Emilia suggested. "He earned himself lots of brownie points with that," Kathy stated.

### Exercise 97

### Having a row

Which reply (a to f) could be made to which sentence with a reproach (1 to 6)?

1. *Are you out of your mind? This is dangerous!*
2. *You have no idea what's going on.*
3. *I can't stand it that you're always ordering me around!*
4. *I never thought that of you.*
5. *What are you trying to say?*
6. *How could you spend all that money?*

a) *That's because you won't tell me anything.*

b) *Well, it appears that you didn't know me very well.*

c) *You know very well what I mean.*

d) *What are you trying to say? It is you who is always telling others what to do.*

e) *It's not as risky as you might think!*

f) *You have no idea how expensive things have become.*

---

64 to listen: (hier) belauschen  65 to overhear: zufällig mitbekommen  66 brownie points: Pluspunkte

"So that's my account of what Christopher Cox was prepared to admit to," David said to Emilia, Robert and Charles a few days later. Charles had, once more, invited them to dinner at the vicarage[67] to celebrate the conclusion of the case. Emilia thought that he was a tiny bit disappointed not to have been involved more. David, however, had told his story so animatedly as if a load had been taken off his mind[68], and Emilia suspected that this was not only due to the fact that Alan Gibson's murderer had been found.

"Would you have got on[69] to Christopher Cox if he hadn't taken a hostage and fled?" Robert wanted to know. "I'm not sure," David replied. "He hid his money very cleverly in offshore accounts and we wouldn't have suspected him because of his lifestyle. His London flat was, if you think about it, more expensive than a flat he could have afforded on the money he earned. But only a very thorough check of his financial affairs would have brought that to light. All we knew was that, one evening two and a half years ago, he and Ivor Byrnes ate at the same restaurant. No, we were lucky that he panicked when Maud went to pick him up."

"And you were lucky that Emilia had developed the theory that made you go to pick him up in the first place," Charles said. "Which was a stab in the dark[70]," Emilia admitted. "It was," David said, "police work sometimes is. And as it turned out you hit the mark."

"But you haven't been able to get a full confession out of him," Robert said. "No," David replied, "we still hope to find the blunt instrument[71] we think he hit Alan Gibson with. Then there would be a chance to convict him of murder. Otherwise, we'll have to see what happens in court."

### Exercise 98

Do your own sleuthing[72]

Having read this book, do you share David's opinion that it was luck that Alan Gibson's murder panicked and that it would probably have been difficult to catch him otherwise?

"Does anybody know how the filming is going to continue?" Charles asked. "Kathy tells me that James has brought in another assistant director

---

67 vicarage: Pfarrhaus  68 to take a load of one's mind: jmd. fällt ein Stein vom Herzen  69 to get on to s.o.: jmd. auf die Spur kommen  70 stab in the dark: Schuss ins Blaue  71 blunt instrument: stumpfer Gegenstand  72 sleuthing (ugs.): Detektivarbeit (to sleuth: schnüffeln)

who he has worked with before," Emilia answered. "She and this new AD have to figure out how best to fill the jobs of first and second AD. It's quite a challenge[73], she says, but they'll manage. And another actor has been found to replace Alan Gibson."

"The film production company," Robert explained, "has decided to reshoot[74] a number of scenes in the gallery." "Does that mean that it will be closed for another couple of weeks?" David wanted to know. "Yes," Robert replied, "but they'll only be returning in February, so there is a chance to sell a few pictures before Christmas. Those shown in the series are to stay in the gallery for the time being, so that there are no continuity[75] problems. Stella says that she's going to make use of the fact that they will be shown on TV. She thinks it might entice customers to buy them."

"So Stella is back?" Charles asked. "She will be soon. Her mother is doing better, I'm glad to say," Robert replied. "And Stella is looking forward to getting to know all the actors," Emilia added, "so I won't be needed any more. But I'll be dropping in sometimes – who knows what will happen?" "Whatever happens is not going not involve the police," David said firmly.

Exercise 99

Find the idioms

Do you know the English idioms or phrases for

*1. aus heiterem Himmel*

*2. das Spiel ist aus*

*3. den entscheidenden Unterschied machen*

*4. ein Schuss ins Blaue*

*5. etw. noch weiter verschlimmern*

*6. etw. spitzkriegen*

*7. nicht die geringste Chance haben*

They can all be found in this chapter.

---

73 challenge: Herausforderung  74 to reshoot: neu drehen  75 continuity (Filmsprache): richtige Anschlüsse (durch dieselbe Ausstattung von Filmszenen)  76 to wrap up s.th. (ugs.): zum Abschluss bringen

Later, Emilia accompanied David to his car. "I understand that you've been to London," she said. "Yes. We were able to wrap up[76] the most important parts of the case on Saturday and Sunday morning, so I went to London in the afternoon. Alix had returned, and I," David gave a smile, "I'm happy to be able to say that she didn't shut the door in my face."

"Your letter must have done the trick[77]," Emilia said. "It seems to have had some effect," David admitted. "But," he grinned sheepishly, "she read me the riot act[78] about clamming up[79] on the phone." "So you and Alix are alright?" Emilia asked apprehensively[80]. "For the moment, we are," he replied and from the tone of his voice Emilia could tell what this meant to him.

"I wish there was something to be done about the distance between London and St Stephen," she said. "We are trying to do something about it," he replied earnestly. "In my letter, I offered to look for a job in London and Alix told me that there is a chance – only a slight one, I think – that her old boss at the hospital in York has a position for her. Alix says that she'd rather live up here."

"I've always had the impression that she doesn't like London that much," Emilia said, "but I've also always thought that you would prefer a big city to this neck of the woods[81]." "Some time ago, I thought so too," he admitted, "but St Stephen has grown[82] on me. Where else would I get my cases solved with so little inconvenience[83] to myself?" Emilia grinned. "You certainly chose the right moment to stay away," she said.

Then she added mischievously, "And who do you have to thank for that? Wasn't it that journalist, I forget her name ..." David groaned. "Cynthia Keefe," he said. "Well, if you and Alix finally get to live together, Cynthia was of infinite use, I'd say. That ought to make her happy – you told me that she dearly wanted to help the police. I wonder if I should give her a call." David groaned again. "Don't you dare!" he said.

---

77 to do the trick (ugs.): seinen Zweck erfüllen  78 to read s.o. the riot act (ugs.): jmd. die Leviten lesen  79 to clam up: nichts (wesentliches mehr) sagen  80 apprehensive: besorgt  81 neck of the woods: (ländliche) Gegend  82 to grow on s.o.: jmd. allmählich ans Herz wachsen  83 inconvenience: Unannehmlichkeit

**Exercise 100**

**Frequently used sentences beginning with "Don't"**

Find the German sentences matching the English ones.

*1. Don't ask. – 2. Don't be a stranger. – 3. Don't be shy. –*
*4. Don't get me wrong. – 5. Don't hold your breath. –*
*6. Don't lose heart! – 7. Don't mention it. – 8. Don't mind me. –*
*9. Don't panic. – 10. Don't push your luck. – 11. Don't worry. –*
*12. Don't you dare!*

*a) Das kann dauern. – b) Frag lieber nicht. – c) Keine Panik. –*
*d) Keine Sorge. – e) Keine Ursache. – f) Lass dich nicht stören. –*
*g) Lass es nicht darauf ankommen. – h) Lass von dir hören. –*
*i) Nur keine Hemmungen! – j) Nur Mut! – k) Untersteh' dich! –*
*l) Verstehen Sie mich nicht falsch.*

# Jane Austen, *Pride and Prejudice* (1813): Plot summary

In early 19th-century England a woman needs to marry – not least for financial reasons, as do the five daughters of the Bennet family of Longbourn near Meryton in Hertfordshire: Beautiful Jane thinks well of everyone; Elizabeth (or Lizzy, the heroine of the story) is pretty, lively and intelligent; plain[1] Mary has taken a religious turn; and Catherine only follows the youngest sister, reckless[2] fifteen-year-old Lydia.

Mrs Bennet (who wants to secure husbands for her daughters) is excited when wealthy young Mr Bingley rents Netherfield, a big house nearby. He has brought his friend Mr Darcy and his snobby sister Caroline, who has set her cap[3] at Mr Darcy. At an assembly[4], likeable Mr Bingley (to the dismay[5] of Caroline) is much taken with Jane Bennet, and Elizabeth is snubbed[6] by Mr Darcy, who is rich and handsome, but obviously thinks Meryton society beneath him[7]. Elizabeth continues to think of Darcy as proud and arrogant, while he, during a visit from Elizabeth and Jane to Netherfield, begins to be very much attracted to her but is too proud to admit to his feelings. They start their verbal sparring[8].

Soldiers are stationed in Meryton, among them charming Mr Wickham, who tells Elizabeth that he grew up at Pemberley, Mr Darcy's grand estate in Derbyshire, and was a favourite of Mr Darcy's late[9] father. He intended to become a priest and old Mr Darcy promised him a living[10] – but the son did not honour that promise, forcing Mr Wickham to become a soldier.

Mr Collins comes to visit, a self-important (and rather stupid) young man, who, however, is financially eligible[11]: As Mr Bennet's male cousin he is to inherit Longbourn and, as a clergyman, he was given a living by Lady Catherine de Bourgh, Mr Darcy's aunt from Rosings in Kent. She wishes him to take a wife, so he intends to marry one of the Bennet daughters.

At a ball at Netherfield, Darcy singles out Elizabeth by dancing with her, it becomes plain that Bingley is on the brink of proposing marriage to Jane, and the younger Bennet girls behave disgracefully[12]. The next day

---

1 plain: reizlos  2 reckless: unbekümmert, leichtfertig  3 to set one's cap at s.o.: versuchen, sich jmd. als Ehemann zu angeln  4 assembly: gesellschaftliche Zusammenkunft  5 dismay: Ärger  6 snubbed: brüskiert  7 beneath him: seiner nicht würdig  8 verbal sparring: Wortgefechte  9 late: (hier) verstorben  10 living: (hier) Pfründe, Pfarrstelle  11 financially eligible: in finanzieller Hinsicht als Ehemann geeignet

the Netherfield party go to London, with no intention to return. Elizabeth is convinced that Caroline and Darcy conspired to separate Bingley and Jane. Jane, who returns Bingley's love, is crushed – as are the hopes of her mother. Mrs Bennet is further enraged when Elizabeth refuses an offer of marriage from Mr Collins, who quickly marries Elizabeth's plain and pragmatic friend Charlotte Lucas instead.

Elizabeth visits Charlotte and her husband in Kent and makes the acquaintance of Mr Collins's overbearing[13] patroness[14] Lady Catherine de Bourgh. At the same time, Darcy and his cousin Colonel Fitzwilliam pay their aunt a visit and Darcy and Elizabeth meet again. He seeks her company, as does Colonel Fitzwilliam, who is himself attracted to Elizabeth, but cannot afford to marry her.

Colonel Fitzwilliam tells Elizabeth that Darcy did his friend Bingley a service by separating him from an undeserving woman – not knowing that the woman concerned is Jane. This only adds to Elizabeth's poor opinion of Darcy, who, the very same evening, finally acts on his feelings and makes her a (rather condescending) offer of marriage. Elizabeth refuses Darcy, and during the ensuing[15] quarrel accuses him of ruining the lives of Wickham and Jane and of behaving in an ungentlemanlike manner.

Darcy leaves, angry and disappointed, but the next day puts a letter into Elizabeth's hands. He was convinced of Jane's indifference[16] to Bingley and did not want his friend trapped in a loveless marriage (Elizabeth admits that Jane does not show her feelings). And he explains his relationship with profligate[17] Mr Wickham, who was neither suited nor willing to become a priest, but returned to Pemberley to claim the (no longer vacant) living. He was compensated[18] by Darcy, gambled away[19] the money and then tried to elope with Darcy's fifteen-year-old sister Georgiana (who has a considerable fortune[20] of her own), an attempt thwarted[21] by Georgiana confiding in her brother. Back in Meryton, Elizabeth is glad that the soldiers leave for Brighton, where her sister Lydia has been invited by the young wife of the Colonel of the regiment.

Elizabeth accompanies her aunt and uncle Gardiner (who live in London) on a journey to Derbyshire, where they visit Mr Darcy's Pemberley estate[22] – a beautiful grand house where everyone speaks well of its owner. By pure chance, Darcy returns home a day earlier than anticipated

---

12 to behave disgracefully: sich völlig deplatziert benehmen   13 overbearing: überheblich, anmaßend
14 patroness: Gönnerin   15 ensuing: sich daraus ergebend   16 indifference: Gleichgültigkeit   17 profligate: liederlich, lasterhaft   18 to compensate: entschädigen   19 to gamble away: verspielen   20 fortune: Vermögen
21 to thwart: vereiteln   22 estate: Anwesen

and encounters Elizabeth. He is as much attracted by her as ever and her opinion of him has undergone a great change.

At the inn where she is staying, Elizabeth receives a letter from Jane: In Brighton, Lydia has eloped with Wickham! At this moment Darcy enters the room, clearly intending to speak to Elizabeth, who, distraught, tells him about Lydia's scandalous elopement. With infinite regret, she sees him leaving shortly afterwards.

Elizabeth returns to Longbourn, while the Gardiners help Mr Bennet look for Lydia and Wickham in London. After some unfruitful searching Mr Bennet returns home – but a letter from Mr Gardiner follows: Lydia and Wickham are found and Wickham is willing to marry impecunious[23] Lydia. It is believed that Mr Gardiner paid Wickham a lot of money, but an indiscreet remark from Lydia and a letter from Mrs Gardiner reveal to Elizabeth that it was Darcy who found Wickham in London, made him marry Lydia and provided money for the newly-married couple.

Bingley and Darcy return to Netherfield. While the relationship between Jane and Bingley blossoms, Elizabeth and Darcy find no opportunity to talk. Darcy leaves for London again, but Bingley proposes[24] to Jane and is accepted. A few days later an unexpected visitor demands to speak to Elizabeth: Lady Catherine de Bourgh has come from Kent to dissuade[25] her from marrying Mr Darcy! A rumour[26] of their engagement has reached Lady Catherine's ears, and in the ensuing heated discussion Elizabeth refuses to comply[27] with Lady Catherine's wish that she not marry Mr Darcy.

Darcy (whom his aunt told about her quarrel with Elizabeth) returns to Meryton and, in more humble words, proposes to Elizabeth a second time. Having overcome her prejudice against Mr Darcy and having come to love him, she happily accepts.

---

23 impecunious: mittellos  24 to propose: (hier) einen Heiratsantrag machen  25 to dissuade: abbringen
26 rumour: Gerücht  27 to comply with a wish: einem Wunsch entsprechen

# Key to the exercises

1. types of film: a, f, j; phases of film production: b, h, i; types of actors' roles: c, k, l; types of texts: d, e, g
2. The sisters are Jane, Elizabeth, Mary, Catherine and Lydia. Jane marries Mr Bingley, Elizabeth Mr Darcy and Lydia Mr Wickham.
3. 1e; 2a; 3f; 4f; 5a, e; 6a, b, c, e; 7b, c, d
4. 1h, 2c, 3j, 4a, 5e, 6g, 7k, 8i, 9b, 10f, 11d
5. more formal: 1, 3, 4, 5; less formal: 2, 6
6. 1d, 2a, 3b, 4e, 5c, 6f
7. biography: *Jane Austen: A Life*; detective story: *Murder at Pemberley*; novel: *Pride and Prejudice*; play: *Hamlet*; science fiction: *Voyage to Planet Austen*; travel guide: *Yorkshire and the North York Moors*
8. Sentences 1 and 3 and sentences 2 and 4 have the same meaning (they would be used with the same people). Sentences 1 and 4 are more formal – full names (or a formal form of address) and more formal expressions are used. In the more informal sentences 2 and 3 first names and less formal expressions are used.
9. 1d, 2a, 3c, 4b
10. 1. I'm delighted to meet you. I've heard so much about you. 2. We're having friends for dinner. I'm looking forward to seeing them again. 3. It's a splendid idea, but I'd rather talk about something else.
11. 1a, 2f, 3i, 4k, 5d, 6b, 7h, 8j, 9g, 10c, 11e
12. 1. Do you know anybody here? 2. How do you know James Riddell? 3. Isn't the weather nice? 4. Have you been to Yorkshire before? 5. What's your name? 6. How do you like the hotel you're staying at?
13. 1h, 2c, 3e, 4g, 5b, 6a, 7f, 8d
14. 1. I'd rather not. 2. just the thing, 3. to return the favour, 4. to make a habit of s.th., 5. to make up one's mind about s.o., 6. to feel out of one's depth, 7. Don't you dare!
15. 1e, 2g, 3d, 4a, 5f, 6b, 7c

16    1. false, 2. true, 3. (mostly) false, 4. true, 5. true

17    I hope that you did not have any trouble to find your way here. – I have never been to Yorkshire. I think that the landscape is simply beautiful. – How do you know Nicholas? I've known him for quite some time. – This is a lovely house. I like how they have done the kitchen. Do you happen to know if Nicholas owns it? – Do you have any children?

18    1. Don't you dare to boss me around! 2. He got into the habit of having a few drinks in the evening. 3. He had gone through a hard time. So the new flat was just the thing.

19    1a, c; 2a, b; 3b, c; 4a, c; 5a, b

20    1. ermorden, 2. sterben, 3. verraten, 4. verhaften, 5. gestehen; idioms: to kick the bucket, to bite the dust, to come clean; phrasal verbs: to do s.o. in, to pass away, to grass s.o. up; to take s.o. in, to fess up

21    5, 3, 7, 6, 4, 1, 8, 2

22    1e, 2a, 3f, 4b, 5c, 6d

23    1. to get out of bed, 2. I see. 3. to send s.o. a text, 4. sheer coincidence, 5. to come up with a plan, 6. to say goodbye, 7. Would you mind?

24    You should have underlined: find out, starting off, let out, going on, call off, go through, put off

25    1. get over, 2. turns out, 3. draw up, 4. go through, 5. step in

26    1. But we have to decide on a strategy in dealing with the press. 2. Could we perhaps hear the police first and then maybe come up with suggestions ourselves? 3. So what would your suggestion be? 4. That sounds sensible. 5. If you think that is going to help, why not? 6. This is important, but I'd be grateful if you informed the actors first.

27    "Jacob Francis says that we will understand that everybody is devastated and that the day cannot proceed as planned. He points out that we will still be able to tour the locations and that in the afternoon we will even be able to speak to a few of the actors. He adds that there won't be any one-to-one talks, however, but another press conference with those of the actors who feel up to it. He does

hope that we understand. He concludes by saying that first James is going to say a few words about Alan, who will be very much missed by everyone."

28 "James Riddell said that filming would resume a few days later. He stressed that nobody could go on at once, but that they had to go on – and that he thought that Alan would have been among the first to say so".

29 1a, 2b, 3b, 4c, 5c, 6c, 7a, 8a

30 1. By sheer coincidence he phoned her shortly before she left the house. 2. David was glad that Kathy acted in a very professional manner. 3. Although he had hardly had time to prepare, he spoke for about thirty minutes.

31 1. He sets up a room at the Swan Hotel to start the interviews, returns to the police station and takes a call from Dr Crewe about the first results of the autopsy. 2. He has found out that the car only crashed when Alan Gibson was already dead. And he has found considerable damage at the back of the dead man's skull. He thinks that this damage was the cause of death, but was not caused by the car crash. 3. He wants to be present at the journalists' meeting with the actors and he intends to begin the interviews immediately afterwards.

32 1. novel, 2. literary form, 3. soap opera, 4. TV format, 5. light entertainment, 6. viewer, 7. filmmakers, 8. story threads, 9. culmination points, 10. suspense, 11. cliffhanger

33 1. He needed some help to keep him going. 2. I have to get to know Mr Gibson. 3. It took him quite some time to recover.

34 You could have asked: 1. Did you see Alan drinking? 2. When did you leave the party? 3. Was there anyone with you?

35 1. He need not have worried that the press conference would not take place. 2. The film production company needed to keep the journalists happy. 3. Jacob Francis had to fend off a number of inquisitive questions.

36 1. Let us go, 2. made him wait, 3. had them repaired, 4. don't let me detain you, 5. allowed him to get up

37 1a, e, g, h; 2b, d, f, g, i; 3c, j; 4b, d, f; 5d, g, i

| | |
|---|---|
| 38 | 1b, d, f, g, k; 2e, h, j, l; 3a, c, i |
| 39 | 1b, 2i, 3f, 4a, 5h, 6c, 7e, 8g, 9d |
| 40 | 1. use: awkward, embarrassing; don't use: precarious; 2. use: good, close; don't use: narrow; 3. use: nice, pleasant; don't use: cute; 4. use: sharply, severely; don't use: cuttingly |
| 41 | 1. three thirty-two a.m., nine nine nine 2. two one, seven oh, three, four; double four, double seven, double two (or: four four, seven seven, two two) 3. eighteen-hundreds; eighteen thirteen, the twenty-sixth of November (or: November twenty-sixth), eighteen eleven, eighteen twelve |
| 42 | 1. to take off, 2. to take a statement, 3. to take fright, 4. to take it easy, 5. to take it for granted, 6. to take pains, 7. to take heart, 8. to take time |
| 43 | 1k, 2d, 3i, 4f, 5j, 6g, 7b, 8e, 9a, 10c, 11h |
| 44 | Suggestions: 1. If you saw something, we'd be glad if you told us. 2. I'd appreciate it if you could find another day for our appointment. 3. I'm afraid that my mobile's battery is flat. Could you give me yours? 4. Would you mind explaining this to me? |
| 45 | You should have underlined "I cannot imagine that …" and "And am I right in presuming that you …" – The criticisms could be rephrased like this: 1. Yesterday Balmaha Entertainment and the police hid the real reason for Mr Gibson's death. This was the reason why we had to make two journeys to St Stephen, which was inconvenient. 2. You wanted to keep the reason for Mr Gibson's death from the media as long as possible. As a journalist, I disapprove of this way of handling matters. |
| 46 | 1. article, 2. tabloids, 3. the society pages, 4. human interest story, 5. to get bad press (in the text: the bad press the police gets), 6. quotes |
| 47 | 1. drag on (sich hinziehen), 2. figure out (herausbekommen), 3. get back (zurückkehren), 4. go together (zusammenpassen), 5. point out (hervorheben), 6. stop by (vorbeischauen), 7. tell off (rüffeln), 8. wake up (aufwachen) |
| 48 | 1c, 2e, 3f, 4g, 5b, 6a, 7d |

49     1. to accommodate someone's wishes – den Wünschen von jmd. entgegenkommen, 2. to disappear from sight – aus dem Blickfeld verschwinden, 3. to gather dust – Staub ansammeln, 4. to give somebody ideas – jmd. auf dumme Gedanken bringen, 5. to have lunch – (miteinander) zu Mittag essen, 6. to hide one's surprise – seine Überraschung verbergen, 7. to raise one's voice – seine Stimme erheben. Eine Wort-für-Wort-Übersetzung ist schon bei so einfachen Redewendungen nicht in allen Fällen möglich, wenn der Sinn erhalten bleiben soll.

50     asap – as soon as possible (pronounce as a word or the separate letters); BAFTA – British Academy of Film and Television Arts (word); 1. aka – also known as (word); 2. CV – Curriculum Vitae (letters); 3. DIY – do it yourself (letters); 4. FAQ – frequently asked questions (letters); 5. MP – Member of Parliament (letters); 6. SOCOs – scene of crime officers (word); 7. TLC – tender loving care (letters); 8. WAG – one of the wives and girlfriends of sports stars (word).

51     Suggestions: 1. Using a bike is eco-friendly and healthy. But using it in the wind and the rain might not be so convenient. 2. You usually take a car if you have to transport heavy items. But the congestion on motorways is getting worse and worse. 3. On a train journey you can relax and look out at the landscape – but it is not so relaxing if the carriages are crowded and you don't get a seat. 4. Taking a plane is often the only way to travel overseas. But you might feel uncomfortable if you suffer from fear of flying.

52     Suggestions: Ivor Byrnes has asked me to help investigate the case. He thinks that we might be able to find out things that the police cannot. David of course thinks that everything is best left to the police. But he had to admit that they haven't made much progress yet. I'm meeting Kathy Cochrane for lunch today. David said that she and Alan quarrelled at the party. I hope that she'll tell me more than she told the police.

53     Don't use: 1a, 2b, 3a

54     These sentences consist of words that are very similar to the German words you would have used in a similar situation.

However, "reeks" means to smell bad; the expression "good appetite" is not used before you begin to eat ("to have a good appetite" means that you can eat very much); "to invite" is typically used when you invite someone to dinner or into your home.

55   1f, i, l, m, p, q; 2a, b, c, e, g, h, o; 3d, j, k, n, r

56   Appropriate words are: 1. for a short time, briefly; 2. quite a bit of, a great deal of, extensive; 3. avid, great; 4. lucky, successful. The other words are not appropriate.

57   1d, 2e, 3f, 4a, 5c, 6b

58   The sequence you should have used the words is: bank statements, debit card, bank accounts, offshore accounts, transferred, cash deposits, inland revenue

59   1. any, 2. any, 3. any, 4. some, 5. some, some, 6. some, 7. some, 8. any

60   1. Klingelt's da nicht bei dir? 2. Hinz und Kunz, 3. Zerbrich dir nicht den Kopf darüber. 4. Tacheles reden, 5. Wie gewonnen, so zerronnen. 6. etw. für sich haben, 7. Du hast vielleicht Nerven! 8. Komm nicht auf dumme Gedanken! – These idioms are not word-by-word translations of the English ones, but some are similar.

61   Direct speech: "I'm looking for Ivor Byrnes and would like to have a look at the rooms the party took place in."; "The receptions rooms will do."; "I have something to do in the kitchen."; "It is a lovely house, but needs to be filled with people. It is to be hoped that not every party will bring about the results the last one has."

62   1. shake your head; 2. nod/give a nod; 3. raise an eyebrow; 4. rolling your eyes; 5. winking; 6. shrug your shoulders

63   Suggestions: 1. Do you have/Are there any vacancies for this weekend? 2. Would a double room with twin beds be available? 3. Does the room have an ensuite bathroom? 4. Does it have a wifi network? I need to write some e-mails. 5. What would the rate for this room be? 6. Is there a special rate if we stay three nights? 7. When can we check in and when do we need to check out by? 8. Could you send me an e-mail confirming the booking?

64   1e, 2c, 3d, 4b, 5f, 6a

65   1. to, 2. about, 3. for, 4. from, 5. with, 6. about, 7. about, 8. for, 9. by, 10. at, 11. out, 12. from, 13. to, 14. on, 15. up, 16. to

141

66 1. David goes to the house near Moreton because he has to speak to Ivor Byrnes as soon as possible. Another reason for his going is that he has not yet seen the house where the party that preceded Alan Gibson's death took place. 2. He is glad to have lunch with her because he needs a respite from all the stressful things he has to do. He also likes Nora – and of course he is hungry. 3. He does not want to ask the famous actor to come to the police station, which could cause journalists to get ideas. He is also glad that he does not have to go back to Moreton.

67 1g; 2f; 3b; 4a, c, e; 5d

68 1. Ivor Byrnes twice withdrew large sums of money from his bank account. 2. Emilia and Nora took advantage of the sunny weather and went for a walk. 3. Nora used to work in a school kitchen. Today, she is a well-known actress.

69 1. don't you? 2. didn't you? 3. did he? 4. have you? 5. can you? 6. won't there? 7. are you? 8. will you?

70 1. village pub, pub crawl; 2. regulars, publican; 3. gastropub, pub grub; 4. pub quizzes, darts, pool

71 1. Sorry! 2. Sorry. 3. I'm so/dreadfully sorry. 4. I want to apologise, I was out of order, I feel really bad about it;
5. I'm so/dreadfully sorry./I feel really bad about it.
6. Excuse me; 7. Pardon?

72 1b, c, e, f, g, i; 2a, d, h; 3j

73 types of phones: cell phone, landline, satellite phone; things to use with a mobile: charger, headset, SIM card; applications on a modern mobile phone: calendar, clock, games; features of an old-fashioned phone: cord, receiver, rotary dial

74 1. eine empfindliche Stelle treffen; 2. auf Schwierigkeiten stoßen; 3. das hat gesessen; 4. zur Flasche greifen; 5. den Tiefpunkt erreichen; 6. an die Decke gehen; 7. sich aufs Ohr hauen; 8. ins Schwarze treffen; 9. sich auf den Weg machen

75 1. oh dear, 2. yum, 3. yuck, 4. sigh, 5. erm, 6. ouch, 7. ah, 8. phew, 9. oops, 10. oi

76 You should have underlined: My thoughts exactly; That might be an idea; Good; 1b, c, e, g, h, k, l; 2a, d, f, i, j; 3a, b, e, f, h, l

77  Suggestions: 1. I my opinion, it might well be helpful. 2. Are you sure that that is a good idea? 3. I think that it's too early to tell if this line of inquiry could be successful. 4. You're plain wrong!

78  1f, 2e, g (also 2b and c, which are less formal); 3a, b, c, d, e, g (g is more formal). In British English, the complimentary close "Yours faithfully" is used if you do not know the name of the person you write to.

79  1. They do not have a special reason, but Emilia thinks it might be good to collect as much information as possible. Some of it might come in useful. Later, they suspect that there might be an accomplice and this information could help identify him or her. 2. He needs to explain to Alix what happened between him and Nora Palliser. Alix does not answer the phone, so he has to see her in person. 3. He is looking for inspiration for his letter to Alix. Emilia has told him that in *Pride and Prejudice* Jane Austen had Mr Darcy write a letter to explain himself to Elizabeth Bennet.

80  1. I'm so sorry that I forgot your birthday! 2. He has screwed up royally. She's really mad/mad as hell at him. 3. I'll do my best to solve this darned case.

81  You should have crossed out: because ~~of~~, ~~being~~ curiously, passing ~~over~~, had ~~been~~, ~~too~~ illegal, ~~to~~ do, throw ~~out~~, drove ~~it~~ off, ~~has~~ had, ~~many~~ ages

82  things related to films and cars: car chase, drive-in cinema, road movie; types of roads: dual carriageway, one way street, toll road; text on traffic signs telling you what to do: stop, dead slow, give way; text on traffic signs telling you what not to do: no waiting, no entry, no stopping

83  1. would rather have slept in, had better not be; 2. had better take along/would rather have taken along; 3. had better drive, would rather not be sick/would rather have driven, had better not be sick

84  1f, 2d, 3c, 4g, 5b, 6e, 7a

85  1. because, 2. before, 3. see you later, 4. great, 5. have a nice day, 6. in my opinion, 7. laughing out loud, 8. thanks, 9. today

86  1. By taking Kathy hostage and escaping the police, it has become obvious that Christopher is guilty. He has to be caught,

and everything has to be done to rescue Kathy. With the police temporarily unable to do so, Emilia and Ivor take up the chase. Ivor has an additional, personal reason: He is in love with Kathy. 2. Maud Johnstone is not exactly thrilled, but she knows that this is the best chance to capture Christopher. So she helps Ivor and Emilia however she can.

87 1. crossroads, junction, roundabout; 2. A roads, B roads, motorways, junctions; 3. bypass, congestion; 4. straight on, turn right, turn left

88 The (relative) pairs of opposites are: arthouse film – B movie, black and white film – colour film, box-office hit – flop, lead – walk-on part, postproduction – preproduction, romcom – splatter film, silent film – talkie

89 1. Emilia was sorely tempted to phone David to ask him if he had finished his letter. 2. Jessica hopes that Nicholas won't be making a habit of throwing parties. 3. Emilia has to restrain herself from asking Ivor too many personal questions.

90 1. The words broadsheet and tabloid refer to newspaper formats, but are also used to refer to types of newspapers. 2. Paparazzi are more likely to work for tabloids. Broadsheets are more interested in serious or investigative journalism. 3. Tabloids often feature glaring headlines and stories about the personal lives of celebrities. Broadsheets generally have smaller headlines and their articles contain more information. 4. Tabloids specialise in sensational stories and often contain gossip columns. If you want to be kept informed about politics, culture and the economy you are better off with a broadsheet. 5. The photos in tabloids often show scantily clad women. Men in business suits are more often seen in broadsheets.

91 1g, 2e, 3f, 4a, 5c, 6d, 7b

92 In the paragraphs above, there are the idioms "out of the blue" and "the pot calling the kettle black". The idioms in the list can be translated with: 1. weiß wie ein Laken; 2. reden, bis man schwarz im Gesicht ist; 3. gelb vor Neid; 4. sich freuen wie ein Schneekönig; 5. wirklich etwas auf dem Kasten haben

| | |
|---|---|
| 93 | The missing words are underlined: <u>was</u>/is a piece of luck; <u>the</u> police, do <u>you</u> remember, dog who/<u>that</u>, <u>has</u> become, pleased about, <u>by</u> the neighbours, <u>that</u> an arrest had <u>been</u> made, whispered <u>to</u> her |
| 94 | 1. intend, 2. escape, 3. intended, 4. pursuing |
| 95 | You should have underlined "I had no idea why" and "he was certain". You're in the know with 4, 5, 8, 9, 10, 11; you're not in the know with 1, 2, 3, 6, 7, 12 |
| 96 | 1d, c, a (a is not very likely, but possible); 2a, c; 3e; 4b; 5a, c |
| 97 | 1e, 2a, 3d, 4b, 5c, 6f |
| 98 | When Emilia first spoke to Christopher Cox (Chapter 1), he claimed not (or hardly) to know Alan Gibson and he gave the same impression in the police interview (Chapter 4). Emma Gill told the police (in Chapter 5) that she first met Alan when they were filming *The Fabulous Fraser Family* – the same film production Christopher told Emilia he had his first real job in (Chapter 7)! So Christopher must have made Alan's acquaintance then. If Emilia and David had had the time to compare notes, they might have found it odd that Christopher pretended not to know Alan Gibson. |
| 99 | 1. out of the blue, 2. the game is up, 3. to make all the difference, 4. a stab in the dark, 5. to make bad things worse, 6. to get wind of s.th., 7. to have a snowflake's chance in hell |
| 100 | 1b, 2h, 3i, 4l, 5a, 6j, 7e, 8f, 9c, 10g, 11d, 12k |